Morecambe Bay Rambles

by

Robert Swain

To Sabre, my faithful companion on most of the walks.

MORECAMBE BAY RAMBLES

ISBN 978-0-9540713-2-5

A catalogue record of this book is available from the British Library.

Published by:
Yan Press, 10 The Nook, Bolton-le-Sands, Carnforth, LA5 8DR.
© Robert Swain, 2008.

Walkers should note that rights of way can be changed, temporarily diverted and, subject to an appropriate order, closed. Permissive paths are not rights of way and the routes can be closed or diverted without warning.

Front cover photograph:
BWC 17 Hampsfell Hospice
Back cover photograph:
BWC18 Eric Morecambe an

LANCASHIRE COUNTY LIBRARY	
11478714	
HJ	26/11/2008
	£10.99

Contents

Page

Introduction
About Morecambe Bay

WALK 1,	Glasson to Lancaster	9
WALK 2,	Overton, Basil Point, Overton	13
WALK 3,	Middleton, Sunderland Point, Middleton	15
WALK 4,	Heysham, Morecambe, Lancaster	21
WALK 5,	Lancaster, Hest Bank, Morecambe	25
WALK 6,	Carnforth, Bolton-le-Sands, Hest Bank, Carnforth via coast	30
WALK 7,	Bolton-le-Sands, Hest Bank, Slyne, Bolton-le-Sands	34
WALK 8,	Carnforth, Bolton-le-Sands, Carnforth	36
WALK 9,	Carnforth, Warton, Yealand, Warton, Carnforth	39
WALK 10,	Carnforth to Silverdale via coast	45
WALK 11,	Carnforth, Warton, Leighton Park, Silverdale	48
WALK 12,	Silverdale Woods, Arnside Tower, Arnside Knott, Arnside	53
WALK 13,	Silverdale to Arnside via the coast	58
WALK 14,	Silverdale to Arnside via Hawes Water	60
WALK 15,	Arnside, Leighton, Silverdale	63
WALK 16,	Arnside, Arnside Knott, Arnside Tower, Arnside	67
WALK 17,	Arnside, Hazelslack, Fairy Steps, Sandside, Arnside	70
WALK 18,	Milnthorpe, Coastal Way, Heversham, Levens Bridge	75
WALK 19,	Levens Bridge, Brigsteer, Whitbarrow, Levens Bridge	81
WALK 20,	Levens Bridge, Whitbarrow, Levens Bridge	85
WALK 21,	Witherslack, Whitbarrow, Witherslack	89
WALK 22,	Levens Bridge, Coastal Way, Lindale or Grange-over-Sands	94
WALK 23,	Grange-over-Sands, Hampsfell Hospice, Lindale, Grange-over-Sands	98
WALK 24,	Grange-over-Sands, Cartmel, Grange-over-Sands	103
WALK 25,	Grange-over-Sands, Hampsfell, Cartmel, Cark	106
WALK 26,	Grange-over-Sands, Kents Bank, Cark	110
WALK 27,	Cark, Flookburgh, the coast, Cark	114
WALK 28,	Cark, Haverthwaite	117
WALK 29,	Haverthwaite, Rusland Pool, Backbarrow, Haverthwaite	122
WALK 30,	Haverthwaite to Ulverston	125

MORECAMBE BAY RAMBLES

Contents   Page

WALK 31, Ulverston circular via Hoad Hill	130
WALK 32, Ulverston, Bardsea, Ulverston	132
WALK 33, Bardsea, Aldingham, Great Urswick, Ulverston	137
WALK 34, Bardsea, Baycliff, Little Urswick, Dalton-in-Furness	142
WALK 35, Aldingham, Gleaston, Newton, Dalton-in-Furness	147
WALK 36, Aldingham, Newbiggin, Leece, Rampside	151
WALK 37, Dalton-in-Furness, Lindal, Urswick, Dalton-in-Furness	155
WALK 38, Barrow-in-Furness, Furness Abbey, Dalton-in-Furness	160
WALK 39, Roose or Barrow-in-Furness, Roa Island, Barrow-in-Furness	165
WALK 40, Isle of Walney	169

Maps
WALKS 1, 2 & 3	20
WALKS 4 & 5	29
WALKS 6, 7 & 8	38
WALKS 9, 10 & 11	52
WALKS 12, 13, 14, 15, 16 & 17	74
WALKS 18 & 22	80 & 97
WALKS 19, 20 & 21	93
WALKS 23, 24, 25 & 26	113
WALKS 27 & 28	121
WALKS 29 & 30	129
WALKS 31, 32 & 33	141
WALKS 34, 35, 36, 37, 38, 39 & 40	173
Morecambe Bay based on OS maps of circa 1850	174

Maps are reproduced from the 1941 Ordnance Survey map. Crown copyright.

INTRODUCTION

All of the walks in this book either touch on Morecambe Bay itself or, at some point, have good views across to the Bay. It is important to remember that several walks can be tidal and advice should be sought locally if in any doubt. It is easy to get into difficulties if the tides are not appreciated. Tide tables can be purchased as a guide, as well, but times of high tide do vary a little from place to place.

All the walks are described as though using public transport. Some of them can be done using bus services alone, some using train services alone and some use both the bus and the train. There is parking near the stations, although sometimes it is limited. It is not a long walk to the bus stops from a place to park, some car parks are by bus stops. The use of public transport gives a much greater freedom to do linear walks.

In Carnforth, the main bus stop for buses from Lancaster and Morecambe and for buses to Warton or Milnthorpe and beyond is on Haws Hill by the station car park, but there is also a service (at the time of writing) from by the station itself. For the Lancaster direction, there is a stop by the War Memorial, which is close to the station. For a stop with further buses to Lancaster and buses to Morecambe, go up New Road, which is reached from the station entrance by passing the Warton/Milnthorpe bus stop, crossing the road and going along a short street to another one where turn uphill to the right. At the top, cross the A6 at the pedestrian crossing and turn left to the bus stop which will have been seen before crossing the road.

At Levens the northbound bus stops are close by Levens Hall on the Grange road and just as the bus turns back eastwards after leaving the Grange road and before going under the flyover. The southbound stop is close to Levens Bridge on its south side and nearly opposite the entrance to Levens Hall.

At Grange-over-Sands, buses stop a few metres from the station, the stop easily being seen from the station entrance.

It is not possible to include train or bus timetables in this book as they keep changing.

All the times given for walks are very approximate and only a rough guide. With several there is much to see and they can take considerably longer than the times quoted, such as if first bird watching on Leighton Moss and then fossil hunting (not to dig them up to take home), bird watching and watching climbers in nearby Trowbarrow.

There can be cattle in fields and occasionally a bull. Make your own

MORECAMBE BAY RAMBLES

judgement on their mood and whether or not it is safe to cross. With one walk where there was a sign for a bull in the field I had already seen the very large gentleman concerned, contentedly lying with his harem on the other side of an electric fence, so was happy to proceed on my way. This would not have been the case if I had been facing him on his own. Cows can be very skittish at times and are particularly likely to be troublesome if you have a dog with you and they have calves. Always be prepared to turn back if you are not certain of your safety or the safety of other people or animals with you.

With all the walks, it is for the persons concerned to ensure their own safety and the safety of their equipment, etc. and no liability is accepted by the publisher or the author for any damages arising from undertaking a walk.

The Bay can be crossed on foot, but this should not be attempted without a guide. The channels can be dangerous and the state of the tide is crucial. An area of sand that looks firm to the inexperienced eye can be quite soft when people attempt to cross it and there are areas of quicksands as well. However, a crossing of the Bay with a guide is normally an enjoyable experience and can be done on a number of days during the summer months, generally for charity. These walks normally start at Hest Bank or Arnside. Cedric Robinson, the Queen's Guide, goes out the day before a walk to check the route and mark it with 'brobs' of laurel. Even then, he checks the river crossings on the day before leading people across them.

Although not specifically mentioned, part of the Lancashire Coastal Way is used in the Lancashire walks. In Cumbria, most of the Cistercian Way is used, as is most of the Cumbria Coast Way from Barrow in Furness.

In doing all these walks, remember you are often going over private property even if it is a right of way or access land. Do not leave any litter. Shut gates after you. Do not cause disturbance to farm stock or damage growing crops, it is the farmer's livelihood. Do not disturb wildlife. Keep dogs on leads at all times; if you meet me my dog will be on a lead. As well as cause trouble if off a lead, dogs themselves can get into unexpected difficulties when on unfamiliar ground and roaming free. Especially take care before passing through fields with livestock when accompanied by a dog or dogs.

ABOUT MORECAMBE BAY

Morecambe Bay is never the same for two days running. Not only does the weather change regularly, but the tides come sweeping in twice a day making for different appearances as well. Changes may be only small from one day to the next at a given time, but after a storm the whole appearance of a part of the Bay can alter. Many tons of sand can then be lifted from one part of the Bay and deposited in another. Storms can also cause coastal erosion, washing into the banks and causing the land to drop into the sea.

In addition, the river channels running down the Bay regularly change, the Kent in particular can move right across the Bay from the Grange shore to the Arnside shore. In 2004 the Keer changed its course revealing the former stone pier at Hest Bank for the first time for over a hundred years, moving vast amounts of sand in the process. Anyone walking on the sands will come to realise that they are not level, but that some areas are higher than others. All this makes for a beautiful and ever changing area and provides a rich feeding ground for many species of birds. For the purposes of this book, Morecambe Bay is being taken as the tidal area extending inwards from a line across from the Isle of Walney on one side to Glasson on the Lune Estuary on the other, although strictly it should go to Fleetwood. Various towns, villages and hamlets that are quite close to, but not necessarily touching the Bay itself, are included. Something of the story of many of these places is told here, as well as describing one or more walks passing through or by them.

First, it will be helpful to learn a little more about the Bay itself. It was not always where it is now. Millions of years ago the area was under a warm, tropical sea. Over time, countless creatures deposited the calcium to make the limestone we see today. Movements of the earth's crust brought the area above the surface, so that at one time it was higher than now. At another time the sea was higher so that areas that are now marshes were under water, making for a number of islands, such as round Silverdale and Arnside.

At the time of the last Ice Age, the whole of the area would be covered in ice and only the tops of the hills would show up above it. Glaciers slowly descended, bringing down rock and debris, some of which formed the drumlins, such as the one on which Lancaster Castle stands and those in Low Furness. As the weight of the ice vanished with the end of the last Ice Age, the land gradually rose, leaving the Bay as we see it today.

MORECAMBE BAY RAMBLES

Man has brought about changes by reclaiming some of the land around the Bay, draining marshes and turning it into agricultural land. The coming of the railways saw further areas enclosed and changes to the river channels.

The sands, the saltmarshes, the inland marshlands, the hills and the woods together with all the other features of the landscape make this a rich area for both wildlife and for plant life.

There can be few places in the country where natural change is so constantly taking place, helping make for the fascination of this beautiful area.

WALK 1, GLASSON TO LANCASTER

Easy.
6¾ miles, 10¾ km.
Allow 2½ hours.

This walk follows the former railway line along the side of the tidal River Lune from Glasson to Lancaster and the bank of the river. It can be very good for bird spotting.

Glasson Dock, as opposed to Old Glasson about half a mile distant, came about through the Lune channel silting up. The Lancaster Port Commissioners passed a resolution to build a wet dock here in 1779, but it was not until 20 May 1787 that the 'Mary' became the first ship to tie up here. She was built in Brockbank's yard in Lancaster.

A dry dock was opened in 1840 and extended in 1852, but sadly this was filled in during 1969 and is now covered with industrial buildings. The gate into the dock lies in the bed at high tide and is raised after the turn to hold the water in the dock. It replaced earlier conventional gates in the 1980's. At certain high tides the water in the dock is higher than the water in the Lancaster Canal basin, resulting in the unusual double gates at the top of the sea lock. The appropriate pair of gates is used depending on which waters are the higher, those in the canal basin or those in the dock.

Formerly, a railway line ran from Lancaster Castle Station to a freight terminus at the end of Victoria Terrace with lines running across the road to what is now a car park by the canal basin. Oddly, the passenger station was about half a mile from the terminus. The line was never heavily used by passenger traffic, but it did once see royalty. On 16 May 1917 the royal train arrived empty whilst King George V and Queen Mary visited a projectile factory. They spent the night on the train, having arrived by car, before departing on it at 8.45 am the following morning, bound for Barrow-in-Furness.

The Lancaster Canal, Glasson Arm was opened in 1826 with the sloop 'Sprightly' passing along it with a cargo of stone from the Duddon, beyond Barrow-in-Furness, to Preston. Vessels had to be demasted to pass beneath the bridges. It is recorded that drinking water for Glasson was taken from the canal basin in 1889.

MORECAMBE BAY RAMBLES

Glasson Church is younger than the canal, by which it stands, it being consecrated in 1840. The Starkie family of Ashton Hall supported the church.

First, there is a small diversion. From the bus stop by the dock, go straight up Tithebarn Hill to the viewpoint at the top, where there is an indicator. On a clear day there is a view all round, from Fleetwood, round by Sunderland Point and across Morecambe Bay, over Basil Point, which has the conspicuous white Ferryman's House, and round to the Pennines. From the viewpoint, return to the centre of Glasson to cross the swing bridge spanning the sea lock which joins the dock to the Lancaster Canal basin.

Follow the road for the few metres to the public toilets where turn left to go by them and onto the riverside path. Follow this path to the right, it being the end of the former railway line from Lancaster and it is part of the Lancashire Coastal Way. Follow the path, over the River Conder, past the stationmaster's house, and come to the picnic area at Conder Green. Continue along the former railway line, seeing Ferryman's Cottage across the Lune. It is a very easy route to follow..

BWM01 Former railway track near Glasson.

WALK 1

On coming to a cottage on the right, there is a tangle of brambles by it covering the site of the old Ashton Hall Halt, a private station for Lord Ashton, of Williamson's table baize and linoleum fame, who lived at the Hall, which now houses Lancaster Golf Club. The right to stop trains was originally granted to Mr. Starkie in August 1883; he was the then owner of Ashton Hall. A red flag was displayed to stop a train.

On reaching the former Aldcliffe Crossing, with the bed of the former railway track continuing straight ahead, turn left along the roadway to the stile at the corner. Cross it and follow the path to the right, along the embankment, not far from the Lune channel. As the path is followed it looks to be going straight to the *Golden Ball* pub at Snatchems, but it and the river channel turn to the right to pass the pub, which is on the far side.

Cross a stile and a few metres ahead is a path to the right to Freeman's Wood. Ignore it and continue ahead along the path for New Quay Road, following the bank of the Lune with a fenced off embankment on the right, which is part of Lancaster's flood defences. As the Quay is approached, the path goes to the right onto the road, which is followed straight ahead towards Carlisle Bridge with the West Coast main line.

Along this stretch of road was the factory of James Williamson and Son. The first James Williamson pioneered the manufacture of table baize. His son took over the business and became an extremely rich man, making many gifts to Lancaster, including the Ashton Memorial that dominates the skyline and the Town Hall. It was he who became Lord Ashton. A narrow gauge railway line ran from the factory to Freeman's Wood, taking ash from the boilers, but it was closed in the 1930's. Over the years, much of the once extensive factory has been demolished so that little now remains. The firm once employed about a quarter of Lancaster's workforce at the various mills it used to operate.

Scaleford Bar, the site of an ancient ford and the lowest crossing of the Lune, is passed on the way to the present lowest crossing, Carlisle Bridge which takes the West Coast main line over the river. Although the bridge itself has been rebuilt twice, the piers are the original ones from 1845. The foundation stone should have been laid on 1 September but was delayed until 25 September because the river was in flood.

MORECAMBE BAY RAMBLES

New Quay, below Scaleford, was built in 1787 because of problems sailing further up the river. St George's Quay, upstream from Carlisle Bridge, was built from 1749 onwards, the year that the Lancaster Port Commissioners were established by Act of Parliament. A number of the quayside warehouses still exist, but have been converted into housing. The older ones are of three storeys whilst the later ones are of five storeys.

Occupying plots 36-38 is the former Custom House which was erected in 1764. Richard Gillow, who was a cabinetmaker and architect, designed it. His firm, Gillow & Co (later Waring & Gillow) imported mahogany from the West Indies and exported furniture, examples of which are found in the 'Judges' Lodgings' Museum at the top of Church Street, near the Castle. Construction was of the best materials and to be in keeping with the best buildings in the town. The four pillars supporting the canopy at the front are each single pieces of stone from a quarry above the town. The weigh house was based in the ground floor and the first floor was occupied by the clerks and housed the Collector's office until 1882 when the customs were transferred to Barrow. There was no internal connection between the two floors until the building was converted into the Maritime Museum which opened in 1985. Subsequently, it was expanded to take in the adjacent warehouse, and is well worth a visit.

Another large Lancaster employer was Storey Brothers, also makers of table baize, who had their mills at White Cross, and which are now part of Lancashire Enterprises. More of the family is told under Bardsea (see Walk 32).

For the bus station, continue straight on along the road, passing the Maritime Museum. For the railway station, turn right at the far end of the Maritime Museum, cross to the far left of the car park and follow the path along to steps up to Vicarage Lane and the Priory Church. From there, pass in front of Lancaster Castle (both of these are well worth a visit), and Castle Park, where turn right for the railway station. Alternatively, turn left for the town centre.

WALK 2

WALK 2, OVERTON, BASIL POINT, OVERTON

Easy.
2¼ miles, 3½ km..
Allow 1 to 1½ hours.

This is a walk round the Lune estuary and is liable to be muddy in places. It visits much of Overton village.

'Overton' is thought to mean 'Shore Town' which is a very good description of this village that dates back to Anglo-Saxon times. It is shown as 'Oureton' in the Domesday Survey of 1086.

St Helen's Church has a fine Norman doorway, but the thickness of the west wall and the use of a different stone suggest that in part it dates back to Saxon times. The church was a chapel to St Mary's Church in Lancaster. The Parliamentary Commissioners reported in 1650 that there were eighty families in the chapelry and that they were six miles from the parish church. They were so surrounded by the sea 'twice in twenty-four hours that they could not pass and had no church nearer than Heysham three miles distant'. The Commissioners prayed for a settled minister and promised to remove the chapel to Middleton, something that did not happen and the church became a parish church from 1765.

Buried in the grounds of St Helen's Church are four river pilots who guided vessels through to Lancaster, very appropriate as the church looks across the Lune.

Some farmers at Glasson held lands across the river in Overton and regularly forded the river by horse and cart at low water, taking across their hay. On 31 December 1806, a farmer got drunk before making the crossing. He was surprised to find that his horse was swimming where it was normally able to ford the river.

At Basil Point is 'Ferryman's House' with a slip down to the beach. Formerly, before the days of the railway, a ferry operated across the Lune between here and Glasson.

BWM02 Ferryman's House, Basil Point.

MORECAMBE BAY RAMBLES

Walk straight along the road from the Overton bus terminus to the centre of the village and then turn right at the junction towards Sunderland Point. After crossing a cattle grid, the road goes up an embankment that is part of the sea defences and continues over the marshes to Sunderland Point. For the walk, turn left away from the road at the edge of the marsh and go along the track, where a sign indicates that it is the way for Basil Point.

The track, from where there are views of the Heysham Power Stations and across the Lune estuary, can be muddy. On coming to two stiles leading into different fields, take the right-hand one to follow the path along the top of an embankment just above the saltmarsh. Cross over a stile and then back onto the head of the marsh, first with a fence on the right and then onto the marsh at another stile. Continue along the head of the beach, which then starts to turn round Basil Point, and onto the Lune Estuary, with Glasson Dock on the other side.

Pass over a stretch of path at the head of the beach, past the Ferryman's House, and along the shore to a little wooden gate by the next houses, through it and up some stone steps. At the top, turn right along the track for Overton, passing through two gateways before coming out onto an unsurfaced roadway, Chapel Lane, and the houses of Overton. Follow the road, perhaps taking a short break to go along to St. Helen's Church down Church Grove, and come to a sign for a footpath to the left by one of the houses.

Follow this good track, passing another path coming from the left, to come out onto a road where turn left for the centre of Overton; then turn right along the road and at the next junction turn left for the bus terminus.

If so desired, Middleton can be reached either by walking along the road, following the bus route for about a mile or, where the road swings left at a bridge at the end of Overton, follow the track straight ahead, by a drainage ditch on the left. A road is reached by going roughly straight ahead, where turn left to the next junction and there turn right for Middleton.

WALK 3

WALK 3, MIDDLETON, SUNDERLAND POINT, MIDDLETON

Easy.
4¾ miles, 7 ¾ km.
Allow 3¼ hours plus time at Sunderland Point.

Many people will tell you that Sunderland Point cannot be visited at high tide, but it can by following this route. It is an interesting experience to arrive there at high tide when the road is submerged.

BWM03 High tide at Sunderland covers the beach roadway between First Terrace and Second Terrace.

The Old Roof Tree Inn dates from 1440 and is believed to be named from the 'cruck' timber construction for its roof.

When Middleton Sands Holiday Camp was popular many people holidayed at such camps, but it has been closed for many years. Various proposals have been put forward for its future use and it is now intended to become accommodation. It was a prisoner of war camp during the war years.

MORECAMBE BAY RAMBLES

From the Middleton bus stops, turn onto Carr Lane, which goes right from the main road just after the stops when coming from the Morecambe direction. A sign indicates that it is the way for Middleton Sands. A bend where Carr Lane swings right is shortly reached and straight ahead is Hallam Lane, the one to be followed.

At the end of Hallam Lane, cross the road in front and the footpath is immediately to the right of the garage of the house. Go along this first, over a stile and then along the right-hand side of the field in front, possibly having to cross another fence on the way. At the end of the field, cross a wooden stile and continue along with the hedge on the right and come to another stile to cross. At the next rather small field, bear left to a stile seen on the other side. (Note, the first field is used twice in this walk. If it too muddy or the walker is nervous of any cattle in it, go back to the road and turn to what has become the left to rejoin Carr Lane and follow that road to its end. An alternative for the return walk is given later.)

After crossing the stile, go left for a few metres and then turn right to follow a grassy farm track along by the right-hand edge of the field. A stile is crossed and there turn left in the next field.

Go along with a hedge on the left, cross another stile and continue straight ahead with the hedge on the left. Come to a wooden stile to cross at the end of the field and a short distance ahead is a further wooden stile at the left-hand corner. Pass down this next field with the hedge on the right. At the end of the field there is a wooden ladder stile by a signpost indicating Middleton and Trailhome. Cross over the stile and along the field with the hedge and fence on the left to a stile leading onto a proper track which is followed to a road.

Turn left along the road and at its end turn left to go along the track at the head of the shore for Sunderland Point. Shortly, as the track turns to go further out over the saltmarsh, leave it to go by the bottom of the embankment on the left. The track is joined again, a farm is passed on the left, after which there is a good track again. In about 200 metres there is a signpost by a field gate indicating the bridleway to the left.

Before using the bridleway, go along to see Sambo's Grave about 100 metres ahead, reached from the beach by some stone steps leading through the wall.

It is not known just how much of the story of Sambo is legend and how much is the truth. It is certain that he arrived on a ship in 1736 and was servant to the captain. The story is that he was left at the inn at Sunderland whilst his master was away on business, intending him to stay there until the ship was ready to sail again. However, Sambo thought that his master had deserted him, fell ill, refused all sustenance, and died a few days later. (It is thought more likely that he caught a fever and died of that.) As he was not allowed to be buried on consecrated ground because he was not a Christian, the sailors around at the time excavated a grave in the rabbit warren behind the village and buried him there.

During the summer months the Rev. James Watson, who was a former headmaster of Lancaster Grammar School ('Royal' status was not granted until 1851), rented a cottage at Sunderland Point. He was told the story of Sambo by George Jackson, the then owner of the inn, and in 1796 wrote an elegy to the former slave. During the course of the summer he collected a shilling a head from visitors, which enabled him to erect a monument to the former servant. Flowers are regularly to be seen on the grave, which looks out across the shore.

On The Lane, passed along after leaving Sambo's Grave, is a small mission church where services are held every two weeks and are arranged according to the tides. There cannot be many churches where the vicar has to refer to tide tables when fixing the times of services.

It is not known when Sunderland Point was first settled, but there could have been very few people here before it became an area known as 'legal quays', where ships could load and unload, in 1680.

William Stout, a Lancaster grocer and wholesale ironmonger, John Hodgson and Robert Lawson, both of whom traded with the West Indies, were some of the earliest traders to use the port. At first the goods had to be unloaded from ships into carts or into lighters for transport to Lancaster. About 1700 a long since gone jetty was built to relieve the problem.

Houses and large warehouses were built at Sunderland, which consists mainly of two terraces, First Terrace and Second Terrace. These have now been converted to residential accommodation. Between the two terraces is a sea wall that has a path for pedestrians along the top of it. Vehicles use the beach below when the tide is sufficiently far receded.

At the end of Sunderland, nearest the actual Point, is Sunderland Hall dating back to 1683. It was here that Robert Lawson and his family lived.

Sunderland once supported two pubs, the Ship Inn at Upsteps Cottage (1 The Lane, where Sambo died) and the Maxwell Arms. They both closed around 1870, but Mrs Wilson of Sunderland Hall continued to sell beer to men who came by boat from Lancaster; she had been the last licensee of the Ship Inn. Boys had to sit at the fish house to warn her of any possible

MORECAMBE BAY RAMBLES

appearance by the police.

Sunderland declined as a port, first with the opening of St George's Quay in Lancaster in 1749 and then the opening of Glasson Dock in 1787. Now it is popular with tourists and local people, most of whom come across the tidal road, which ends at "The Anchorage", the first house passed on arriving from Overton.

From Sambo's Grave, return to the bridleway, The Lane, and go straight along it to its end at Sunderland. Follow the roadway to the right if going to see Second Terrace and Old Hall. For the main walk, turn left and come to the tidal road across to Overton. Instead of using the road, pass "The Anchorage" and continue along the head of the shore for about 100 metres to a stile by a signpost. From the stile, strike diagonally right across the field, roughly in line with the Power Stations at Heysham, pass under the pylon line and, in the corner is a wooden footbridge leading to the next field, crossing over one dyke and by another.

Turn right in this field to go along by the dyke to another wooden footbridge. Cross it and the farm track on the far side and continue straight ahead, still with a ditch on the right. Another footbridge is crossed at the end of the field, where turn leftwards to the far right corner where there is a wooden ladder stile to cross, close to an embankment. Cross right over the field, fairly close to the hedge on the left until reaching wooden steps which are near the corner.

The path then goes just above a farm track to another wooden ladder stile, leading out onto the embankment, where turn right. Just before reaching a field gate, drop down the embankment to a further ladder stile. There, the right of way actually cuts straight across the corner of the field to a bend in the farm track. Join the good farm track and go straight along it, passing the farm buildings to the right.

The track becomes a tarred roadway and then comes to a small stile on the right leading onto a concrete roadway. Cross it and turn left and then at the end of the field previously being walked a wooden ladder stile leads back onto the tarred roadway, and turn right. Follow the track along and take the one to the right where it splits at Trumley Farm. Pass along the edge of the farmyard, through a field gate and onto a farm track. A few metres ahead another track crosses, but it is ignored unless using the alternative ending, and continue towards Middleton ahead. At the next field, entered at a field gate, the right of way goes across the farm track and then straight ahead to rejoin the track, which has curved round the right-hand side of the field.

WALK 3

Continue straight along the track by a ditch on the right, ignoring a nearby field gate.

Shortly, as the field is crossed, there is a corner which drops down to the right. There, cross a wooden ladder stile and then follow the grassy field path by the fence and ditch on the right. A wooden footbridge leads across the ditch and from it bear towards the far left corner of the field by the houses of Middleton. This is the field used at the beginning of the walk. On reaching the corner, cross the stile and follow the path to the road, which is crossed, and pass straight up Hallam Lane.

Go up Hallam Lane, across the junction and onto Carr Lane on the far side, turn right for the bus stop, which is just to the left from the top of the road.

For the alternative ending to this walk, which avoids using the first field twice, turn right onto the other path a few metres beyond Trumley Farm. Follow the path straight across two fields and out onto a minor road where turn left. The road comes out at the bottom of Overton village. Go up the street to where the road for Morecambe goes off to the left and follow it down to the bus terminus. If parked at Middleton and not using the bus, continue straight along the road.

By using the tidal road between Sunderland and Overton this walk and the previous one can be linked. It is vital to remember that the road should not be crossed unless there is sufficient time to do so on a rising tide. People have been trapped trying to cross in vehicles as well as on foot. The deepest part of the flooding is at the Sunderland end of the road.

MORECAMBE BAY RAMBLES

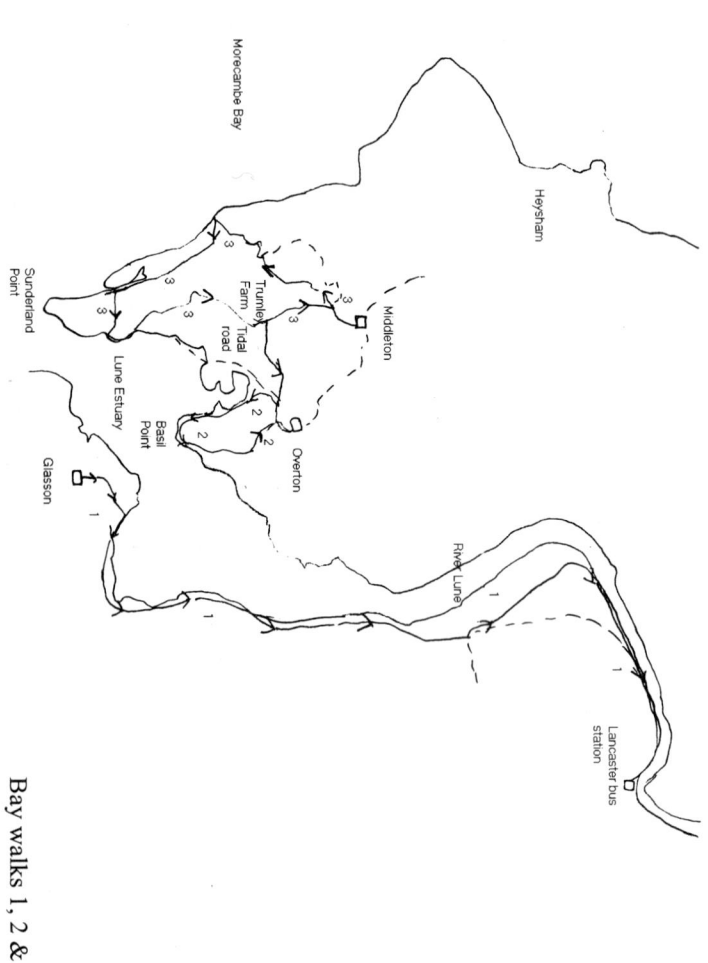

Bay walks 1, 2 & 3

20

WALK 4, HEYSHAM, MORECAMBE, LANCASTER

Easy.
7¼ miles, 11½ km.
Allow 3¼ to 3½ hours.

This is a pleasant walk mainly on the promenade by the shore before turning inland to follow an old railway track through to Lancaster.

Heysham is in three parts. Heysham Harbour is the port for passenger and cargo ferries, its official opening being on 1 September 1904. By it are the two nuclear power stations seen from many parts around Morecambe Bay and the gas field support base. The harbour is still served by a rail passenger service, but it is a far cry from the time when "The Ulster Express" was an important train running to the port from London Euston. The Lancaster, Morecambe and Heysham electric railway line terminated at Heysham. There were extensive railway sidings. Heysham was the first port in the country to be operated by electricity.

Higher Heysham is the main residential part of Heysham. It has Heysham Old Hall, which was completed in 1598 and is now an inn. The building was at one time uninhabited and due for demolition, but was bought by William Barker, a Lancaster brewer, in 1956 and converted into the inn two years later.

Below is the old fishing village. "Lade End" must have seen many fishermen go down here to launch their boats. That was at a time before the promenade round to Morecambe had been built. No doubt many would be regulars at the "Royal Hotel" on Main Street.

On the headland above are the remains of St Patrick's Chapel with the adjacent stone coffins cut into the living rock. Below, nearer the village, is St Peter's Church. It is believed that both buildings were originally constructed around the same time. Viking graves have been found around St Patrick's Chapel.

A hog-back gravestone stood outside St Peter's Church for many years, but it is now inside the church to preserve it from erosion. The church was extended in 1864, when the north aisle was added. A blocked up doorway shows changes in the building as its height outside is different from its height inside the church.

Oddly, at one time Heysham was in the Kendal deanery although it was detached from the main part of it.

MORECAMBE BAY RAMBLES

BWM04 St Peter's Church, Heysham.

At Higher Heysham there is a special bus bay that buses normally use and forming the main stop. From it, cross the road towards *Old Hall Inn* and turn left to walk along the road for a few hundred metres to Smithy Lane, where turn right. Follow the road down and round to the left, where there is a car park over to the left. There, two signposts close together indicate paths, the one needed being the farther one, for Lade End, and go out onto the shore. Turn right and follow the shore for about 100 metres and then go up some steps and turn left along the field at the top.

Pass through a wooden kissing gate leading onto Heysham Head and follow the path along above the beach. Stay on that path (there are various paths here and using any should get you to the right point, but the one described is closest to the Bay) until the Sandylands Promenade area of Morecambe comes into view in front. Turn right and follow the grassy path up to the ruins of St. Patrick's Chapel on the headland.

There are other ways down from the Chapel, but it is suggested that the cobbled roadway by the rock graves and the ruins is followed, passing the car park by St. Peter's Church below. Drop down to the main village street and turn left away from the shops. Go down the road and just round the corner is a signpost for the footpath to Whinnysty Lane on the left. The path turns right onto the bottom of the sea defences.

WALK 4

Sandylands Promenade is part of Morecambe's sea defences against the encroachment of the tides. It was because of storm damage here in October 1927 that Heysham Council merged with its more powerful neighbour and the promenade was built. At the end stands the 'Battery' hotel. It gets its name from the time that an artillery battery stood in front.

The Midland Hotel is the second building to stand on the site and is named after the Midland Railway Company. It is well-known for its art deco design of the 1930's; the architect was Oliver Hill and the design is based on an ocean liner. The hotel has featured in 'Poirot' on TV.

Opposite the Midland Hotel is the former Promenade Station that now houses the Tourist Information Office and 'The Platform', where a variety of entertainments are held. As a station, it was the end of the Midland Railway line from Yorkshire, and it was also used by the former Lancaster and Morecambe electric train service, which also served Heysham. The electric service was one of only three electrified sections on the former Midland Railway and was used for experiments as it was remote enough not to interrupt important services. As late as 1958 it was used between Carlisle Bridge and Oxcliffe Bridge for experiments in connection with the electrification of the West Coast main line. The last of the electric trains ran into Morecambe on New Year's Day, 1966. Now, the former railway line is a walk and cycle route to Lancaster.

The Stone Jetty originally took trains, which had to cross the promenade to reach it, causing traffic problems at the level crossing over Marine Road. The Jetty was part of Morecambe Harbour, which operated until the opening of Heysham Port in 1904, when all the staff, equipment and trade were transferred to the new facilities. The lines ran along the jetty to the station, which is now a café at its original end. Following the closure of the harbour, the site was used by the Sheffield firm T W Ward Ltd, whose ship-breaking yard operated there until they finally left on 26 July 1933. Now, the Stone Jetty is part of the 'Tern Project' connected with birds and is a very popular stroll.

Roughly opposite the Stone Jetty and a close neighbour of the former Promenade Station, is the Victoria Pavilion, commonly known as 'The Winter Gardens', which was built on the site of a former baths and opened in 1897. There were financial problems over the years and the building changed hands a number of times before closing its doors in 1977. Famous names, including Laurel and Hardy, George Formby and Billy Cotton had all performed here. 1962 saw a very successful season with the Black and White Minstrel Show.

MORECAMBE BAY RAMBLES

The Grade II* building is now owned by a trust who are hoping to restore it to use as a multi-purpose venue.

Morecambe is, of course, famous as birthplace of Eric Morecambe. Since his statue on the promenade was unveiled by Her Majesty the Queen on 23 July 1999, countless visitors and others have had their pictures taken with him.

From the start of the walk in Heysham, simply go straight along the promenade for about two miles. As the Stone Jetty and art deco Midland Hotel are approached, leave the promenade and cross the pedestrian crossing about 100 metres before the hotel (1). Once across the road, turn left and at the road junction turn right along the road, which is part of the Lancashire Coastal Way.

At the roundabout ahead cross straight over and turn right a few metres along Hillsmore Way and see the path to the left to follow. The path goes by the railway with the line on the left, passing the station on the way. Follow the path under a road bridge and shortly come to a road where turn left to cross the single-track line to Heysham. Follow the pathway for around 35 metres to a road, which is crossed, and go diagonally left to the cycleway and walkway along the old railway line. The route is tarred and has streetlights and is simple to follow. Pass under the main West Coast railway line at Carlisle Bridge.

Go up to the road and then drop down again onto the walkway by the river to the Millennium Bridge in front. Cross the bridge (2), taking the branch to the right to drop down to St. George's Quay, where turn left for the bus station.

The Millennium Bridge is the latest crossing of the River Lune, it being opened in March 2001. Its design is based on a picture of a ship in the Maritime Museum. It has some unusual features, one being that it is not actually fixed to the sides of the riverbank or quay so as to allow movement with changes in temperature. The bridge is roughly on the site of the medieval bridge which spanned the Lune. The original line of the road for the north was in front of 'The Three Mariners' pub and across the river .

Close by the end of the bridge is the memorial to the Slave Trade that various Lancaster vessels operated between Africa and the West Indies.

1. Walk 5 joins here.
2. Walk 5 joins here.

WALK 5, LANCASTER, HEST BANK, MORECAMBE

Easy.
8¾ miles, 14 km.
Allow 3½ hours.

A very pleasant walk using riverbank, canal and coast.

The station was formerly known as 'Lancaster Castle' to distinguish it from 'Lancaster Green Ayre'. The 'Lancaster and Carlisle' line opened in 1846. The castle and the Priory church tower above their much younger neighbour.

The first fort on the top of the hill was built by the Romans, who had arrived around 70 AD. They built three forts here over the years. Church Street of today was the civilian settlement and several finds from Roman times have been found along its length. Below St Mary's church are the remains of an old Roman bath house that were excavated and preserved when the car park behind was built.

Hadrian's Tower and the Norman Keep date back to around 1093. The Gatehouse was built around 1400 AD by the future Henry IV, John o' Gaunt's son. The statue of John o' Gaunt was placed above the gate in 1822. Much rebuilding work of the castle took place in the late 1700's, the architect being Thomas Harrison. He was responsible for both the magnificent Shire Hall and the Crown Court, which is still in regular use. The castle housed Lancashire's only assize court from 1362, when it became the seat of the assizes.

BWM05 Millennium Bridge, Lancaster.

MORECAMBE BAY RAMBLES

Lancaster Castle is famous for having housed the so-called Pendle Witches before their subsequent trial and execution on the moor above the town. Another prisoner who endured very uncomfortable privations was George Fox, the founder of the Quaker movement.

It is probable that there was some place of worship on the site earlier, but there is no known detail before St Mary's church, the parish church of Lancaster, was founded by Roger of Poitu in 1094. Monks from his hometown of Seez in France ran the church. During the reign of Henry V in 1414 the church was handed to trustees and became the parish church, saving it from destruction at the time of the Reformation. The tower was built in 1759 to a different design from the main church building. It replaces an earlier tower that had become unsafe after being increased in height and the extra weight of further bells being hung.

Greyhound Bridge formerly carried the electric railway line from the nearby Green Ayre station to Morecambe. It is the third bridge to take the railway line across the River Lune, the first being built on of piles of timber, the second being of iron and built in 1864, whilst the present bridge was built 30 feet below the earlier ones in 1911.

Green Ayre refers to a large green area by the river Lune and across to Cable Street. The station occupied what is now largely a green area again. The turntable was close to the roundabout by the supermarket.

Upstream from Green Ayre is Skerton Bridge of 1788, which was built to replace the medieval bridge for traffic to and from the north. It is another of Thomas Harrison's works and was the first bridge in the country to be built with a level road deck rather than arched. The bridge has five elliptical arches and was built at a cost of £14,000.

The former railway line passes beneath the right-hand arch of the magnificent Lune Aqueduct taking the Lancaster Canal across the river It is 600 feet long, 60 feet high and has five arches. The piers are Gothic in shape above the bed of the river but are rectangular below. Masons' marks can be found on the side of the pier by the former trackbed. The arches are constructed of dressed stone up to the huge cornice. It was designed by John Rennie and built by Alexander Stevens and Son of Edinburgh. The piers were completed by June 1795 at a cost of £14,792.49 and the whole structure for £48,320.94, rather more than the originally estimated £18,608.80. It would have cost much less if it had been built of brick, as Rennie originally intended, rather than of stone as was insisted upon by the Lancaster Canal Company directors.

WALK 5

From the ticket office entrance to Lancaster station, turn left to go up the path to the road, where turn right for a few metres. Cross the road at the top of the hill and go straight along by the castle, with it on your right, and then into the grounds of the Priory Church. Continue straight ahead, past the church tower, and drop down the path beyond, passing the way to the Roman Bath House on the right. At a flight of steps and a slope for the disabled, it comes onto a former railway track where turn right to cross a bridge.ABstract Pass the Millennium Bridge (2) and a road to the right leading to the bus station. At the end of the track, by Greyhound Bridge, go along the road for a few metres to reach the way down to the underpass on the right.

On coming out of the underpass, turn left to the walkway by the River Lune and follow it along, passing under Skerton Bridge. Continue along the track, passing Skerton Weir and then to the Lune Aqueduct seen spanning the river ahead. There, turn right to go up the steps onto the Lancaster Canal towpath and turn left to cross the aqueduct (3). Continue along the towpath for about two and a half miles until the boats and the centre of Hest Bank are reached. (See Walk 6 for some information about Hest Bank.)

Drop down the steps to Station Road (4) and straight down it, across the pedestrian crossing over the Morecambe road and to the former Hest Bank station. Cross the railway line and onto the foreshore where turn left to follow the Lancashire Coastal Way at the head of the shore. As some houses are reached, the path goes straight in front of them and then in front of the Leisure Club, past the car park and as you come to a roadway there is a footway to the right by the sea defences.

On reaching the promenade, turn right and follow it along by the sea defences for nearly two miles. On the way, it becomes part of the main Morecambe promenade. Pass the lifeboat station, the clock tower, and the Eric Morecambe statue. Instead of going straight along, on reaching a car park, turn right to continue round at the edge of the Bay and come to the head of the Stone Jetty. Pass it (or enjoy a stroll to the jetty at its end and back) and round the Midland Hotel and a hundred or so metres beyond (1) there is a pedestrian crossing over the road. Cross it, turn left to the nearby road junction where turn right. Go along the road, passing bus stops, and cross straight over the end of Hillsmore Way at the roundabout to reach Morecambe railway station and more bus stops.

For the centre of Morecambe, cross the pedestrian crossing by the station and then follow the road round to the shopping precinct.

MORECAMBE BAY RAMBLES

On following this walk, Bare is the first of the villages to be reached that was to become part of Morecambe. In many ways it still has its own village atmosphere with its row of shops curving inland from the sea front. After the closure of the artillery battery at Morecambe's West End, it moved to Scalestones Point in 1886. The soldiers were part-timers of the Leeds Artillery and came every summer for a number of years. At that time, there was no road to Hest Bank and only fields where there are now the golf links. Happy Mount Park opened at Whitsuntide in 1927.

After passing various hotels and guesthouses, Morecambe Town Hall is seen on the left. Its foundation stone was laid in 1931, the building being erected to house the council of the recently joined boroughs of Morecambe and Heysham. Following its opening there was a ball at The Tower, which was then its neighbour and has long since been demolished. Close by are streets that were fishermen's cottages, part of Poulton(-le-Sands), a village that was to become a part of Morecambe and close to its present central area. Poulton Square is a reminder of the former village.

The Clock Tower has stood looking out across the Bay, by the site of the former Central Pier, since 1905.

1. Walk 4 uses this route to Hillsmore Way.
2. Walk 4 joins here.
3. By turning right, the towpath can be followed to a bridge near to Lancaster Town Hall from where the city centre can be reached.
4. Walk 6 also goes down this road.

WALK 5

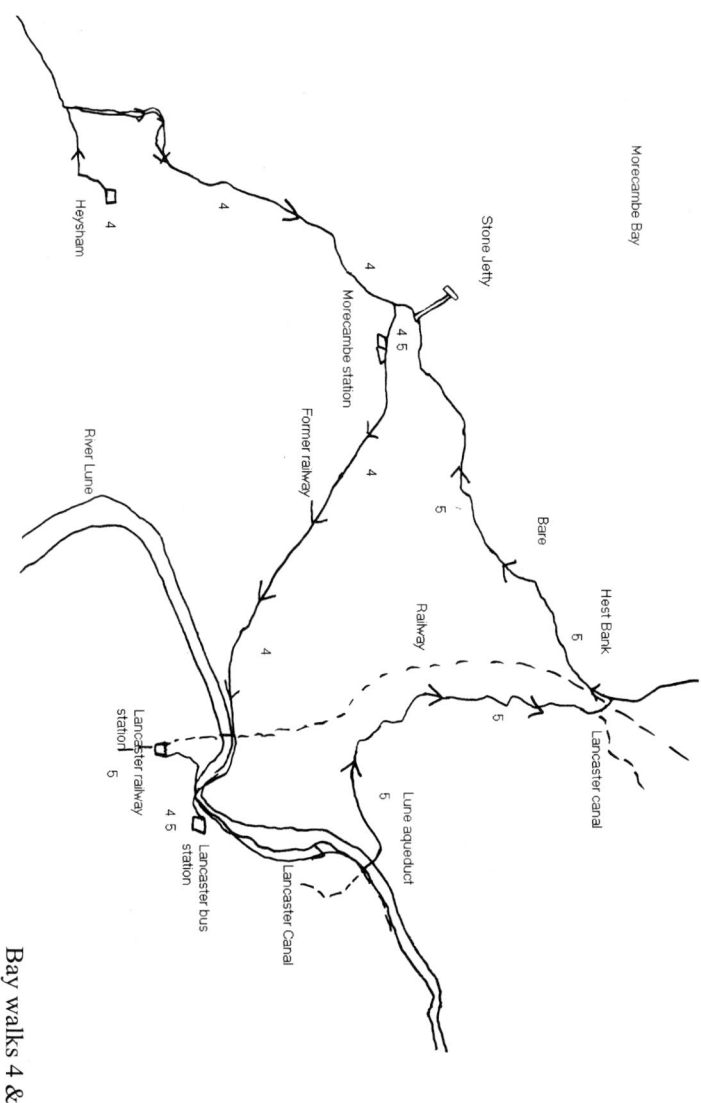

Bay walks 4 & 5

MORECAMBE BAY RAMBLES

WALK 6, CARNFORTH, BOLTON-LE-SANDS, HEST BANK, CARNFORTH VIA COAST

Easy.
9¼ miles, 14¾ km.
Allow 3 ½ to 4 hours.

Whilst described as being from Carnforth station, this walk can just as easily be done from Bolton-le-Sands or Hest Bank. It is a mix of canal towpath and head of the beach and is subject to tides.

In the early 1800's, Carnforth was a rural township and was part of Warton parish. Its main street was along what is now North Road, which was then the main turnpike road through to the north. In 1820 the new turnpike road by-passed the old main street of Carnforth, and is now the main A6 used by countless vehicles every year. As late as 1851, Mannex directory shows Carnforth as having only three inns, two shoemakers, a joiner, a tailor, a blacksmith and one shop, all the rest of the businesses being farms.

The opening of the Lancaster Canal in 1797 had not had a major impact on Carnforth, no settlement being built around it, but it had provided work for local people in three gravel pits then owned by the Lancaster Canal Company. Now, another former sand and gravel pit is part of Carnforth the extensive Carnforth Marina. Opposite the marina is the 'Canal Turn' public house, which was originally the stables and house.

Carnforth station is famous for featuring in the David Lean film 'Brief Encounter', starring Trevor Howard and Celia Johnson. It has been extensively restored in recent years, having been allowed to become very run down. The central platform now houses a museum and 'Brief Encounter, is regularly shown. The refreshment room has been restored as in the film and is very popular. The clock has been restored and ticks steadily away. Unfortunately, trains no longer call at the main line platforms but there are regular services round the coast for stations to Barrow-in-Furness and also some to Leeds.

The town developed following the coming of the railways in 1846, when the Lancaster and Carlisle line was opened through Carnforth. In 1857 the Ulverston and Lancaster Railway line came to Carnforth, the start of it becoming an important junction. The Midland Railway line to West Yorkshire followed in 1867. Each of the companies had its own engine shed and yard.

Along Warton Road is the wall of what was the Carnforth Iron Works that operated from 1864 to 1929. It was in a triangle formed by Warton Road on one side, the main line on the other side and the Furness and Midland joint line at the top. Accommodation had to be built for the workers and about a hundred houses were built at Millhead. Bessemer Steel was produced at the site until 1889, there having been six blast furnaces. Production of iron continued, but steadily decreased until the closure of the works in 1929.

From the station entrance, go straight ahead to the road, by a bus stop, and turn right up to the top of Haws Hill. At the main A6, turn right to the junction by the supermarket and cross over it at the pedestrian crossings and turn right. On reaching the *Canal Turn* pub join the canal towpath and turn right.

On reaching a bridge over the canal (5), cross it and turn right to follow the path by the canal. See the remains of a bank of five coke ovens on the right. Pass through a metal kissing gate, along by the canal and then bear left over the grassy pathway up the field to another metal kissing gate. This is actually part of the original turnpike road. Follow the track up to a roadway and then pass along it until a bridge over the canal is reached.

Do not cross the canal, but turn left up the steps and then right along the path at the top. Follow that main path round through the wood and out into the open where it is between two fields. The path comes out onto a roadway, Mount Pleasant Lane (6). Turn right and follow it to a junction and to the right is the centre of Bolton-le-Sands. Cross over the main village street and go down St. Michael's Lane, over the canal bridge and onto the towpath, where turn right (7) for Hest Bank.

BWM06 Jumbo Rock, Bolton-le-Sands.

Bolton-le-Sands was originally called 'Bolton', but with the coming of the railways in particular it became necessary to distinguish it from other places of the same name and, in particular, the Lancashire mill town of 'Bolton-le-Moors'. It dates back to Anglian times, the name referring to a farmstead.

The village was much changed with the coming of the Lancaster Canal in 1797. The road from Hest Bank was cut at Town End, resulting in a new road having to be built to connect with the turnpike road from Lancaster, which dates from 1751. Packet Hill was built to take the turnpike from the centre of the village to its old line. The original road ran to the right of the Packet Boat Hotel and is now known as Packet Lane. The houses to the right below Packet Hill are on the line of the old road.

According to Mannex Directory of 1851, there were 'some extensive malting establishments and three respectable inns'. There are still three inns, the Blue Anchor and the Packet being unchanged. The Black Bull stood behind the bus stop close to the Blue Anchor and has now been converted to housing. For many years it was the local Co-operative store. The other present inn is the Royal Hotel on the A6 at the Carnforth end of the village. Nearly opposite it is the ancient pinfold, which was cut by the road being improved, from when stray animals were impounded for collection by their owners.

Bolton-le-Sands station was demolished many years ago, a victim of the Beeching Axe. Farmers used to take their milk down to the station in large metal kits in time to meet the milk train. The crossing was manually operated and it sometimes happened that a train was held at the signal whilst a farmer with his trailer of hay crossed the line.

Holy Trinity, the parish church, was earlier dedicated to St Michael and now has a chapel dedicated to that saint. It dates back to Saxon times, but much of the interior is from alterations in Victorian times.

It was from Hest Bank that coaches made their way across Morecambe Bay to Kents Bank at low tide. However, travellers crossed that way for many years before the first passenger service started to operate in 1781. The Hest Bank hotel was used by many such travellers and had a powerful lamp in one room to guide them on their way after dusk.

Hest Bank is the only point of the West Coast Main Line where the sea is to be seen. The station was another victim of the Beeching Axe and is now used by businesses. The signal box, which replaces an earlier one, remains in use for controlling the crossing onto the shore.

From the top of the footbridge, the former Hest Bank Pier or wharf can be seen at the edge of the shore other than at high tides. It was built in 1820 to allow small vessels from Glasgow and Liverpool to discharge their cargoes for onward transportation along the Lancaster Canal. For many years the pier had been lost to view beneath the sands so that nobody knew of its continued existence until the River Keer changed its channel in 2004 and removed vast quantities of sand, bringing it into view again.

It was only in 1933 that the Coastal Road between Bare and Bolton-le-

WALK 6

Sands was opened. There was a road, Hatlex Lane, to Bolton-le-Sands, which ended at Hest Bank station.

Follow the towpath along for a mile and a half to the boats at Hest Bank. Turn down the steps and pass straight down Station Road. Cross over the Morecambe road at the pedestrian crossing to reach the railway (4), over it and turn right along the roadway. Where it forks, take the left-hand path to go along just at the head of the shore. Pass Jumbo Rock, which is a large erratic left by a retreating glacier at the end of the last Ice Age.

Pass below Red Bank and then Red Bank Farm and onto the sea defence. Walk straight along it and at the end drop down some steps. Continue straight on along the path to a road. The road is followed for a few metres until taking the turning to the left of Wild Duck Hall, the farm in front.

As the road swings right to Bolton Holmes Farm, leave it and carry straight on along the path at the head of the shore. There is actually more than one grassy path that can be followed, all going in the right direction. Part way along the grassy area between the head of the sands and the stones at the head of the shore becomes quite narrow. There are several channels to cross along the way. Ahead see the red face of Crag Bank with Warton Crag beyond.

The grassy area becomes broad again and the path is followed towards the white shingle in front. On reaching the shingle to the right of Crag Bank, turn left to follow the Lancashire Coastal Way. Go amongst the rocks, grass, etc. to round Crag Bank and come to a small waymarker indicating that the path is a little further out from the Bank.

The path goes towards Marsh House Farm and then bears away to the left of it, some waymarkers showing the route, but a number of channels making the way not as straight as they suggest. Keep on along the path and after leaving the farm come to the head of the shore, a little way from the Keer channel over to the left. Go through a little wooden gate and then follow the track at the head of the grass, some little distance from the river channel. The path comes out at a stile by a field gate and onto a road, which is tidal. There, go straight along the road, passing a wooden footbridge (8), and at its end onto the Carnforth to Warton road, where turn right for Carnforth Station.

4. Walk 5 also goes down the road.
5. Walk 7 continues straight along the canal bank.
6. Walk 7 also uses this road.
7. Walk 7 also uses this stretch of canal towpath.
8. Walk 8 crosses the footbridge.

MORECAMBE BAY RAMBLES

WALK 7, BOLTON-LE-SANDS, HEST BANK, SLYNE, BOLTON-LE-SANDS

Easy
4 miles, 6½ km.
Allow 1¾ hours.

A mix of towpath, minor roads and field paths.

From the centre of Bolton-le-Sands, where there are bus stops, go down St. Michael's Lane, over the canal bridge and onto the towpath, where turn right. Pass under Town End Bridge and the next bridge is Hatlex Swing Bridge. Continue on along the towpath to Hatlex Bridge, (from where Slyne can be reached by crossing the bridge and following Hatlex Lane ahead). For the walk, continue along the towpath to the next bridge. Leave the towpath and cross the bridge. Pass the *Hest Bank* hotel and at the road junction by there turn left along Peacock Lane.

   At the end of Peacock Lane there is Hatlex Lane coming from the left, changing its name to Hanging Green Lane going to the right. Turn right for Slyne and follow the road to a junction where go to the left of the church. Follow the road, now Manor Lane, to the A6 in front. There, cross diagonally left to Bottomdale Lane and go up it.

   Pass the entrance to Slyne cemetery and come to a metal kissing gate on the left. Pass through it and go diagonally right across the small field to a wooden stile leading onto the football pitch. Cross straight over (or go round if a game is in progress!) to a wooden kissing gate and then across a narrow section of a field and through another metal kissing gate into a small plantation. Follow the path along the edge of the plantation, through a wooden kissing gate into a field and straight across it, fairly close to the hedge on the right, to a metal field gate in front.

   The field gate leads out onto Ancliffe Lane. Turn left to go down to Bolton-le-Sands, coming out at the centre of the village just over a mile distant.

WALK 7

Slyne is an ancient royal manor and appears in the Domesday Book. The village was formerly a township, Slyne with Hest, in the parish of Bolton-le-Sands. Slyne with Hest is now a separate parish.

In a corner opposite the Cross Keys hotel are the ancient stocks where wrongdoers were imprisoned.

The old coaching route across Morecambe Bay passed along what is now Hest Bank Lane. Until 1751 it was a rough way that had been used by the monks of Furness Abbey visiting their Beaumont Fishery on the River Lune, but that year became a branch of the Garstang and Heron Syke Turnpike road.

BWM07 Hatlex Swing Bridge, Lancaster Canal, Bolton-le-Sands.

MORECAMBE BAY RAMBLES

WALK 8, CARNFORTH, BOLTON-LE-SANDS, CARNFORTH

Easy.
5¾ miles, 9¼ km.
Allow 2½ hours.

A very pleasant walk involving canal towpath and countryside.

From Carnforth station entrance, follow the roadway out to the main shopping street in front and go up it, passing the shops. Cross the main A6 at the pedestrian crossing and continue up the road, Kellet Road, ahead to where there is a bridge over the Lancaster Canal. By it, turn right along the path through the children's playground and onto the canal bank, where turn right.

Go along the towpath, passing the Carnforth Marina, under Thwaite Bridge (5), the first of five to be passed beneath before reaching Bolton-le-Sands. Either leave the towpath here to pass the shops and two of the pubs or continue to the next bridge, which is crossed up to the village centre by St. Mary's Church.

There, pass by the church with it on your left to go up the road for Nether Kellet. In about 150 metres, by the village school turn left along Mount Pleasant Lane (6). Follow it to a crossroads of roadway and paths and there turn right to go past a row of cottages, Tarn Cottages.

BWM08 Bolton Church Bridge, Bolton-le-Sands.

WALK 8

The track is followed for about 200 metres to where there is a wooden stile by a field gate leading into the field on the right. Cross it and go up the field, fairly close to the hedge on the right, to an outward corner of the field in front. There, cross a wooden ladder stile into that field. Go up the field, which has good views back to the Bay and Lakeland Fells, by the hedge on the left and come to another wooden ladder stile leading out onto a track.

Continue along the track until an unsurfaced roadway by the motorway is reached and there turn left to come to a stile by a field gate. Cross it and go diagonally right over the grassy path up the hillside in front. Follow the path more or less in the direction of a pylon seen ahead, through a plantation, until two successive wooden stiles leading through a hedge are crossed. Go over the next field to another wooden stile in the right-hand corner.

That stile leads into a plantation, where follow the path ahead. The first part is an open area, which is crossed, and as the end is reached the path goes right into the trees and then turns left to come out again at the far side. Cross the open area in front and go up to a metal ladder stile. From it, drop down the field diagonally towards the far left-hand corner. There, cross a metal ladder stile and go round by the fence on the right to another metal ladder stile to cross into a field.

Cross the field to the far right corner, go over the stile there, then a farm track followed by another stile. From it, turn to the left to go diagonally across the field to a stone squeeze stile to the left of a field gate. Cross the farm track at the other side to another stile into a field and go down by the hedge on the left. Again, there are good views of the top end of the Bay and the Lakeland Fells.

At the end of the field a stile leads out onto a track, where turn right and follow it, through two field gates and over the canal bridge. Once over the bridge, join the towpath and turn left. Follow it to the *Canal Turn* pub and come out onto the A6 where there are bus stops. Turn right and cross the road at the supermarket. Continue along the A6 for a few more metres and then drop down Haws Hill on the left and at a junction come to the railway station and other bus stops at the bottom.

Walk 6 crosses the bridge.
Walk 6 uses the road in reverse.
Walk 6 also uses this stretch of canal.

MORECAMBE BAY RAMBLES

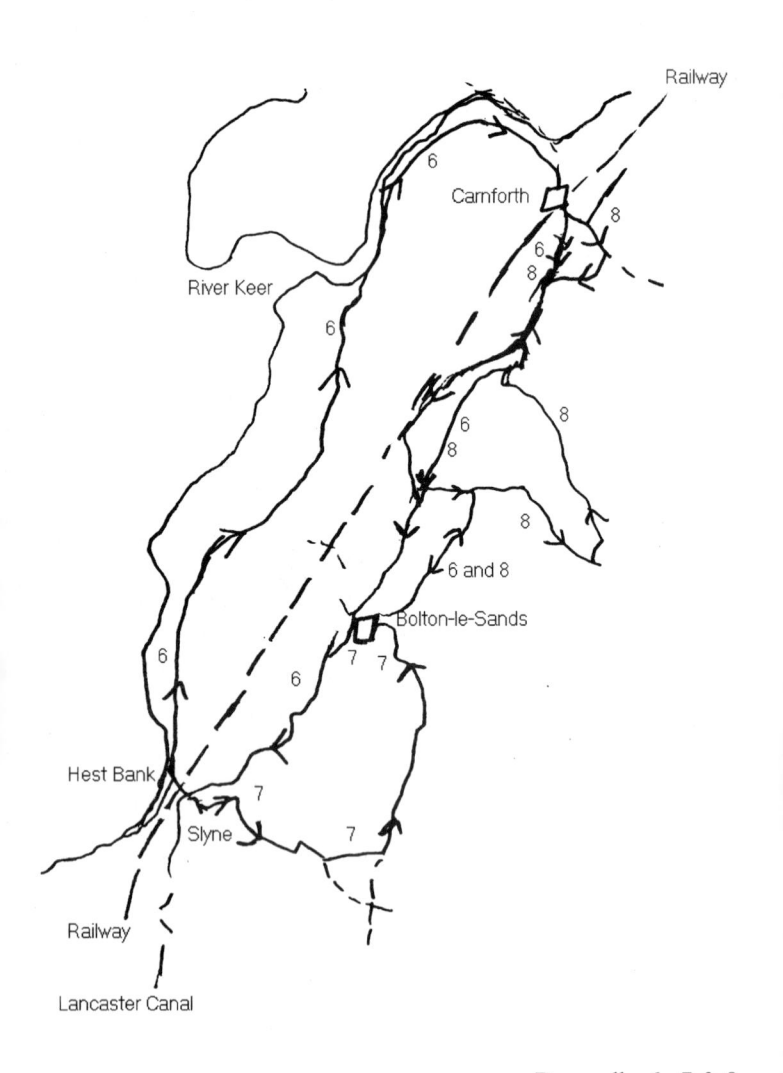

Bay walks 6 , 7 & 8

WALK 9

WALK 9, CARNFORTH, WARTON, YEALAND, WARTON, CARNFORTH

Mainly easy, but parts of the ascent of Warton Crag are moderate.
10 miles, 16 km.
Allow 5¾ hours.

Ascend a limestone crag and wander through woodland.

From Carnforth station entrance, turn left along the road to cross the railway bridge. Follow the road along by the railway to the first turning on the left after going under one bridge and reaching another. This minor road goes by the River Keer and then comes to a wooden footbridge on the right (7). Go over it and continue up a road on the far side. At the top of that road, turn right and go straight along it into part of Warton. Pass the garage and on coming to the first of the main houses of Warton to the left of the road there is a farm track going off to the left by them.

Turn up the farm track and at its end pass straight up the field in front, by the hedge on the right to reach a stone stile out onto a road, turn to the left. Ignore a kissing gate on the right, but continue along a little further to a large wooden field gate on the right. Go through it and up the track in front. The track starts off initially going to the left, but very soon turns and then comes to a bend where there is a junction. There, take the more grassy track going to the right. On reaching a corner of the fence just in front, turn left and go up the path, cross a wooden stile, and keep on climbing up Warton Crag.

The path goes over a rocky area and then turns to the right to come to the fence above the former quarry. A few metres before reaching a stile seen ahead there is a good path going off to the left (9). Follow this path up the hillside (you can go over to the left to some perched rocks, but have to return to the path again), crossing another path and then coming to a stile in front of the rock face which is ascended. At the top of it another path is crossed and continue straight on up the Crag. An easier rock face is climbed to come out onto the summit plateau.

There are two possibilities of the origin of the name of Warton. One is that it may refer to the 'Weir', the site of a former tarn, by The Malt Shovel inn in the village. The other is that the name comes from 'the Weard', meaning 'a watch place', by the town. The latter description would refer to the hillfort of the Brigantes on the top of Warton Crag. Dates for the fort range from 600

MORECAMBE BAY RAMBLES

BC to 100 AD. It covered an extensive area and the limestone cliffs formed a natural barricade. Traces of the ramparts curving round the summit plateau are still to be seen. The hillfort is a Scheduled Ancient Monument.

The crag is limestone country with cliffs, terraces and limestone pavement. It is the habitat of rare plants and butterflies as well as common ones. All four fritillaries have been found on the Crag.

Follow the path in front, passing to the left of the beacon and the triangulation pillar and come to a junction, where there is a signpost (8). Take the path to the right and follow it down to its end at the unsurfaced Occupation Road. Turn right for a few metres to a stile by a field gate on the left. The next section is a permissive route and may be closed on certain days of the year (in which case continue down the Occupation Road to its end and turn left along the Coach Road).

Cross the stile and turn right along the track as it goes to a wall and then passes along, generally close to it. On coming to a corner in the wall the diversion to the three large rocks which form the 'Three Brothers' can be taken. To visit them, turn left along the earthen path and in a few metres come to an indicator post showing that the route is to the left, into the woodland. Shortly, the three rocks, standing in a line are seen. The permissive path, which is indicated, goes right round them. Return from there to the original path.

Keep on along the very clear permissive bridleway and follow it round to a stile by a field gate and onto the Coach Road, where turn left. The road passes the main entrance to Leighton Hall, which can be visited when it is open, and about three hundred metres beyond there is a stile on the left leading to the path for Summerhouse Hill viewpoint. Follow the good path along to the viewpoint, which looks down onto Leighton Hall and across Leighton Moss and Morecambe Bay.

From by the viewpoint, turn right to go through the gateway and straight along the grassy path over the field. Pass the circular stone mound that is the remains of the summerhouse and then go down the path straight in front. On getting close to a field gate (11) turn left to go up the hillside to the left of Yealand Manor, then seen in front, and follow that path through a metal gate into the woodland.

Just after passing the end of the Manor, there is a field gate with a wooden gate just to its left to pass through and then continue straight along the path across the field. At the end of the field (12), go through the squeeze stile by the field gate. Just after the stile there is a fork; take the left-hand path into

WALK 9

the woodland. On reaching a signpost, continue straight on ahead. At the next junction take the path to the right and drop down it to a fence where turn left along by a fence bordering a field, and then turn left again. It is a clear track to follow and shortly goes through a field gate.

There are two endings to the path, either of which can be taken. As the track bends to the right, there is a path straight in front. Either go along that path or turn right down the track and past some houses. Both endings come out onto the road at Yealand Redmayne, about two hundred metres apart, where turn right.

Leighton Hall is open to the public in the summer months. It was once owned by Thomas Worswick, who was a former Lancaster banker. He sold it to Robert Gillow, the father of Richard Gillow. The Gillow family were Lancaster cabinetmakers and various items of Gillow furniture are to be seen in the hall. It is still owned by descendants of the Gillow family and open to the public in the summer months.

The Yealands appear to have been just one district and are shown in the Domesday Book of 1086 as 'Jalant'. There are three of then, Yealand Conyers, Yealand Redmayne and Yealand Storrs. Yealand is pronounced 'Yelland' and refers to the Anglo-Saxon for high land.

In Yealand Conyers is the Quaker Meeting House, which is the oldest place of worship in the villages. It was built in 1692 and has an old mounting block at the entrance. George Fox had preached in Yealand in 1652 and from then Richard Huddlestone, who became a friend of Fox and one of his strongest adherents until his death in 1662, organised secret meetings in private houses.

Below houses on the eastern side of Yealand Redmayne are fields that formed part of a medieval field system before the Parliamentary Enclosures of the 18th century. Families had unfenced strips each a furrow long in an open field system. Each of these strips was worked by a peasant and, in addition, there was common land for use by all. At the bottom of the fields is the old Back Lane from the village well, now a public footpath.

The road is followed through Yealand Redmayne to where the road for Milnthorpe goes off to the left. Turn down it and at the bottom of the field on the right there is a stone squeeze stile leading into it. Cross over the narrow field, the first of a medieval field system, to a squeeze stile into the following field and similarly into a third field. In the fourth field, bear diagonally to the right for the kissing gate into the next field. Cross this field and a sixth field, where go through a squeeze stile with a metal gate and along a lane between fields to a field gate in front.

Come out onto a roadway and turn left for the stile by the field gate spanning it. Cross to the stile by the field gate on the right of the roadway and then bear diagonally left to the squeeze stile by the field gate in front. Again bear diagonally left over the field, seeing what used to be a Drovers' Pool to the right from the days when the drove road followed this route. Cross a wooden fence stile and then a squeeze stile into the corner of the following field and go across it by the hedge on the right. This area tends to be muddy.

At the end, by a field gate, there is a little wooden gate to go through and a few metres beyond a similar gate leads onto a lane which is followed to a road. Cross the road to go along Church Lane, passing St. John's Church, and at its end cross over the road to the track in front. At the end of the lane, by Dykes House Farm, there is a wrought iron gate on the right, leading into a field. Go up the field and see how some houses cause the right-hand part of the field to extend further than the left. Go just to the right of the houses and then through a wooden gate leading through a gap in the wall and out onto the road where turn left.

Pass through part of Yealand Conyers (the *New Inn* pub is to the right if refreshments are needed), round the corner by the Roman Catholic Church, and just by a field gate on the right there is a stile to cross. Follow the path up the grassy slope to the right and at the limestone outcrop in front turn left (13). Do not go up the good track ahead, but turn left to a small gate leading into Hyning Scout Wood, where there are several paths that can be followed. A suggestion is to use the right-hand fork where the path first splits and go along it, through a gap in a wall, and continue along to a fork from which fields can be seen ahead. There turn left go through another gap in the wall and drop down the path in front to another junction, where turn right to a squeeze stile through the wall and out onto a track and then turn left.

At its end, the track comes out onto the road again. Turn right to go through Warton. Pass through much of the village to come to a bus stop by *The Malt Shovel* (14). Turn left and go over the grass area and then onto a footpath going to the right. At its end, cross the road towards another path between two dwellings. Follow that path, through a metal kissing gate and along the field by the hedge on the left. At the end, pass through another kissing gate and cross the small field beyond to a further kissing gate and out onto a roadway.

WALK 9

The roadway is followed to its end and then turn left along the road from Warton to Carnforth, which is followed to Carnforth station and bus stops.

If you are in Warton on 4 July, you will see the Stars and Stripes flying from the tower of St Oswald's church and probably meet some Americans. Now inside the tower, but outside until 1955, is a stone of the Washington family coat of arms. It has three mullets and two bars and is said to be the inspiration behind the United States flag.

St Oswald's church is the parish church of the village and is dedicated to the second Christian King of Northumbria who became a convert on the Isle of Iona. At one time this was the mother church of a very much larger parish that included Carnforth and Silverdale.

Across the road from the church are the ruins of an old rectory built in the early 14th century. It had a large hall off which were a buttery and a pantry plus a passage to the kitchen. At the time it was built, the Manor Courts were held here, later being transferred to The Malt Shovel.

BWM09 The Old Rectory, Warton.

MORECAMBE BAY RAMBLES

Washington House on the Main Street was the home of a branch of the Washington family from County Durham, of which there were many members in the area.

Behind Main Street is Back Lane, which was a cattle route to pastures behind the village. Here, there is the village school, replacing a building close to the church.

The road up the Crag, passing along the side of the George Washington pub is the old road to Silverdale. The oldest of the quarries on the Crag is on the right and is now a car park.

8. Walk 6 comes along this road on its way to Carnforth.
9. Walk 10 also uses this path to the summit.
10. Walk 10 uses the path to the left.
11. Walk 11 also uses this stretch of path.
12. Walk 11 turns left here.
13. Walk 11 goes to the right.
14. Walk 10 goes up the road on the right.

WALK 10

WALK 10, CARNFORTH TO SILVERDALE VIA COAST

Moderate.
5½ miles, 9 km.
Allow 3¼ hours.

Visit part of Warton Crag and then drop down for a walk at the edge of the shore.

From Carnforth station entrance go up to the roads in front and turn left to cross the railway bridge. Follow the road under two railway bridges and over the bridge spanning the River Keer. A few metres beyond there turn right along a roadway passing in front of some terraced houses. At the end of the roadway pass through a wooden kissing gate and then straight across the field in front to another wooden kissing gate. Once through it, cross the field by the hedge on the right to reach the first houses of Warton. At the end of the field, there is a metal kissing gate and then a short track to the road in front, where turn right. After about 40 metres there is a path going off left from the other side of the road. Follow the path round and come out onto the main road through Warton at a bus stop (14).

Cross the road and go straight up Churchill Avenue to where it turns left. There, follow the path straight ahead, go through a wooden kissing gate and then straight up the field. At the top there is a stone squeeze stile onto the road, which is crossed to Ged's Gate diagonally to the left. From the gate, go straight up the stony path between the trees. On coming into the open at the top of that stretch, take the path to the left; it comes onto the limestone pavement.

Go along the pavement, bearing right onto a higher level, because it is easier to walk, and continue upwards to a stile above the old quarry. A few metres beyond the stile, take the path going to the right (9). Cross another path leading to the perched rock to the left and continue onwards and upwards over the rocky limestone path as it goes up a cliff face. At the top, continue straight ahead, crossing another path on the way. Go up a smaller limestone cliff and out onto the summit plateau of the Crag with its views across Morecambe Bay, Arnside Knott and Hawes Water near Silverdale.

Cross over the plateau using the path passing to the left of the beacon, ignoring the triangulation pillar to the right. On reaching a junction, take the left-hand path, there is a signpost indicating that it is for Crag Foot. Go through a wooden gate and continue straight ahead, ignoring the path to the

MORECAMBE BAY RAMBLES

Coach Road to the right. Come out by a field gate onto what is known as the 'Occupation Road' and turn left. This track comes out onto a road, where turn right and drop down to the junction at Crag Foot. Continue along the road towards Silverdale for about 200 metres to where it swings to the right. There, take the roadway to the left for Jenny Brown's Point.

Pass under the railway bridge, follow the track to the right, over a small bridge, and then go through a field gate and turn left along the path, which is actually on the top of a reclamation embankment. The path continues along the embankment as it bends round and then crosses a stile (16) onto the mainland again.

Turn left along the head of the shore to pass the well-known chimney. Continue along the rocks or along the shingle, and there is some sand as well, at the head of the shore. Pass Brown's Houses on the right and see the end of a road just ahead. Go up onto the road, and follow it for about 300 metres where turn into Jack Scout on the left.

Take the more coastal paths in Jack Scout, where there are a number, until the path turns inland. It shortly comes to a junction, where take the right-hand path, its leading to an old lime kiln. Go to the left of the kiln and out onto Lindeth Road again, where turn left. Pass a road junction for Wolf House Gallery(15) and continue straight on into Silverdale. If going into the village centre, turn left onto the road for Arnside. If going to the station, on leaving Lindeth Road carry straight on ahead down the road for Carnforth, Stankelt Road, and, on coming out at a junction turn left for the short distance to the station.

It is generally said that the chimney at Jenny Brown's Point is the sole remaining building of copper smelting taking place here, copper having come from mines on Warton Crag. However, it has also been suggested that the chimney was a beacon for guiding vessels around dangerous quicksands. Close by is Brown's House. Said at one time to have been an inn.

Jack Scout is well known for its abundance of limestone flowers. Here is a former limekiln from the days of producing burnt lime. It has been restored by the National Trust and was fired, when people were surprised at the vast amount of smoke produced.

Below Jack Scout is Cow's Mouth, up which cattle were driven after they had crossed the sands of the Bay. Coaches once used this route onto the dry land.

WALK 10

This walk can be linked with Walk 13 by turning left down Shore Road a few metres before the turning for Carnforth and Silverdale village centre.

9. Walk 9 also uses this path to the summit.
10. Walk 9 uses the path to the right.
14. Walks 9 and 11 use the path from Warton to Carnforth.
15. Turn left here for joining walk 13 to Arnside to this one.
16. Walk 12 goes up Heald Brow by this stile.

BWM10 Walkers by chimney, Jenny Brown's.

MORECAMBE BAY RAMBLES

WALK 11, CARNFORTH, WARTON, LEIGHTON PARK, SILVERDALE

Moderate, but only for a short stretch, otherwise easy.
5¾ miles, 9¼ km.
Allow 3½ hours.

Use farmland, woodland, limestone country and moss land on the way to Silverdale.

From Carnforth station entrance go up to the roads in front and turn left to cross the railway bridge. Follow it along, under two railway bridges and over the bridge spanning the River Keer. A few metres beyond there turn right along a roadway passing in front of some terraced houses. At the end of the roadway pass through a wooden kissing gate and then straight across the field in front to another wooden kissing gate. Once through it, cross the field by the hedge on the right and come to the first of the houses of Warton. At the end of the field, there is a metal kissing gate and then a short track to the road in front, where turn right. After about 40 metres there is a path going off left from the other side of the road. Follow the path round and come out onto the main road through Warton at a bus stop (14), where turn right.

Whilst the road through the village can be followed for about a mile, it is suggested that this alternative be used to where the route enters woodland at a field gate. Roughly opposite the church entrance there is Back Lane between the houses, a signpost indicating it is the way to the Village Hall. Go down there and follow Back Lane to its end, cross Borwick Lane onto Chapel Walk and go along it to the farm. There turn right here to follow the grassy track through the field, pass an old limekiln and just after it turn left onto another track passing above the kiln. Leave the field at a metal kissing gate by a field gate and turn left along the road up to the main road, where turn right.

Pass the last of the houses on the left and come to a stile by a field gate on the left leading into Hyning Scout Wood. Go along the track through the woodland, passing a stile on the way, to a field gate and continue through the wood beyond it. The track becomes a woodland path which is followed to a squeeze stile with a little gate into a field. Go through it and turn right along the field. Continue ahead, ignoring the path dropping down to the right (13), with parts of Yealand to be seen through the trees. At the end there is a wooden kissing gate and then a few more metres of woodland before coming out onto a road at a stile by a field gate.

WALK 11

Turn right along the road for about 150 metres and, at a bend, there is a squeeze stile on the left into woodland. Just inside it there is a signpost and the path to be taken is the one to the right for Yealand Redmayne. A short way ahead there is a gateway that is ignored, and instead turn left in front of another signpost close by and onto a path going towards Yealand Manor (11), which is to be seen in front. The path does not go to the Manor, but a little way up the hillside above it and comes to a metal gate leading onto a path going through the woodland.

Go along the path and just after passing the Manor there is a gateway on the right with a little gate by it leading into a field. From it, follow the track along the field, which narrows at its end (12). There, turn left to cross a wooden stile over a fence and then go up the rocks in front. At the top there is a path to follow, it shortly going through a very small wooden gate and turning left.

Shortly, the path turns right to drop down into Deepdale. This stretch can be slippery as it goes quite steeply down over limestone rock and care should be taken. At the bottom there is Deepdale Pond with trees all round it. Follow the path quite close to the pond and then up a good track, and turn left. Ahead the main track swings to the left, but the walk follows the woodland path straight in front. On coming to a gate into a field, go through it and turn left. From along here there are views across to the top of Leighton Moss.

Continue ahead, through a field gate opposite and then bear a little to the right down the field to its very end by Leighton Hall Farm, where there is a field gate out onto a roadway, and turn right (17). Follow the roadway along, pass Grisedale farm, through a field gate, and at a junction take the right-hand track for the Moss. The track then turns towards to the Moss, goes through a field gate and passes straight across the causeway. On the way across, there is a public hide from which to observe the birds.

On reaching the road at the far side of Leighton Moss, turn right for a few metres to a small wooden gate by a field gate on the left. Go through it and take the permissive path to the right for Trowbarrow.

Leighton Moss is a major RSPB reserve. The land was originally moss land, but was drained and converted for cultivation in the early 1800's, the work being funded by a grant during Napoleonic Wars.. It had to be pumped to keep down the water, but the tide did occasionally break through. Following a dispute over payment to keep the pumps working, the land was allowed to flood again in 1913. Now, it is maintained so as to provide a wetland habitat for the many birds that are either resident or visit it annually.

MORECAMBE BAY RAMBLES

The name 'Trowbarrow' refers to a trough or gully and a small hill. It is this trough which is followed into the former quarry. It was formed by the erosion of a bed of soft mudstone and is bounded by limestone cliffs. Whilst this is the clearest section to follow, the trough can be traced through to Sandside.

The limestone rocks were deposited around 340 million years ago. They are very rich in fossils which have been exposed by quarrying. The most common ones are of fossilized excreted materials from creatures that burrowed below the surface of the sediment on what was then the sea bed. These fossils are sausage like lumps on the rock surfaces.

The proximity of the Furness Railway line just to the west of Trowbarrow meant that stone could easily be transported by rail. The quarry was working until 1959. For a few more years, tarmacadam, a process of mixing crushed limestone with hot tar brought from Carnforth gasworks, continued there, where the process was pioneered. The works buildings were demolished in the 1970's. Now, the area is popular with geologists, naturalists and climbers, there being over a hundred listed routes of all grades.

BWM11 Shelter Stone, trowbarrow, a shelter when blasting rock.

WALK 11

Pass a signpost for the right of way, which crosses over the path, and then come to a metal gate in memory of John Mabson, a musician and climber and continue ahead into woodland. The path shortly turns right and comes to a welcome sign for Trowbarrow Local Nature Reserve, which is actually entered at own risk.

Pass the signboards and then take the left-hand path where it splits. This leads down into the main part of the former quarry. Turn left on reaching it, towards the stone blocks across the entrance and a gate for vehicles. Follow the track straight down out of the quarry and come to a notice board at the end, near the railway. By it, turn left along the path to the line, which is crossed with care and then go straight up the field to a wooden ladder stile out onto a road. Turn left for Silverdale station about a third of a mile away.

11. Walk 9 also uses this stretch of path.
12. Walk 9 leaves here.
13. Walk 9 comes up this path.
14. Walks 9 and 10 also use this path.
17. Walk 15 is joined here.

MORECAMBE BAY RAMBLES

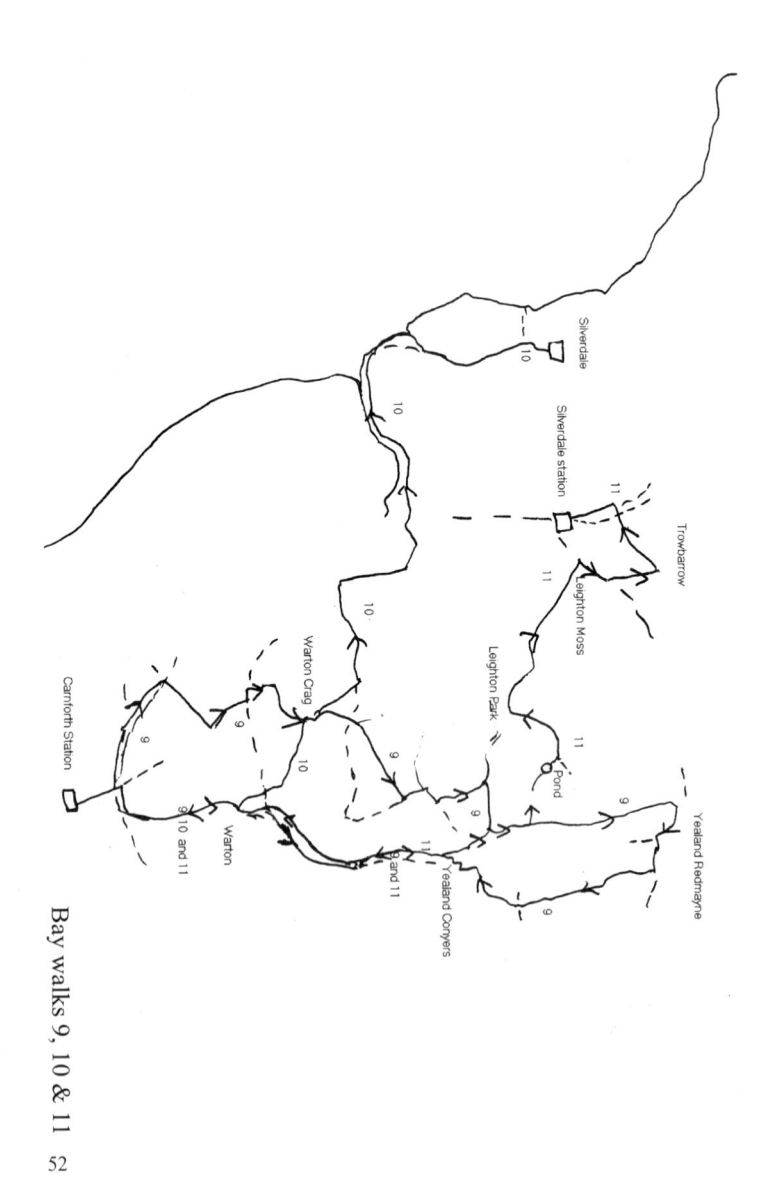

Bay walks 9, 10 & 11

WALK 12, SILVERDALE WOODS, ARNSIDE TOWER, ARNSIDE KNOTT, ARNSIDE

Easy unless the limestone is slippery.
6¾ miles, 10¾ km excluding the diversion to the Pepperpot.
Allow 4½ hours.

A lovely walk with a lot of limestone land and woodland.

Silverdale was a chapelry in the parish of Warton, but is now a parish in its own right. It has several attractive houses, including round 'The Green', just off the road for the station.

In Victorian times it was known as a watering hole and steamers used to call here. Then the beach started to silt up and a very extensive saltmarsh was formed. However, by the 1980's the tides had again started to reclaim the marsh, revealing at times the posts where fishermen had earlier staked their nets. By the shore is a row of cottages formerly occupied by fishermen. Much of the saltmarsh in front of them has now been eroded, revealing broken pots and other items dumped here in the past.

There are a number of ancient wells in Silverdale, including Woodwell where the water drips out of the rock cliff. It is said that it falls as rain on Warton Crag, passes beneath Leighton Moss, and then comes up to the surface again here.

From Silverdale station, turn left along the road for a quarter of a mile to the junction for Carnforth and Silverdale village, taking the village road on the right and shortly come to Hollins Lane on the left. Follow Hollins Lane for about 200 metres and then turn left onto a track, a signpost indicating that it is for 'Jenny Browns'. It is a very clear path to follow, leaving the woodland and having reclamation fields to the left with a view across to Crag Foot and Warton Crag, and ahead to Morecambe Bay.

The path comes up to the reclamation embankment. Just before it there is a wall where, without going through the gateway, turn right (16) to go up Heald Brow. Follow the clear, grassy path upwards and to the left to come to a stone squeeze stile. From there, follow the clear main path ahead through the woodland, over a limestone step and to a waymarker, where turn right onto some open land. There, see a stone squeeze stile taking the path through the wall in front.

From the stile, go along by the wall on the left, passing over two fields and

MORECAMBE BAY RAMBLES

at the end cross a stile at a corner of a small tongue of woodland. From it, go through a small wooden gate out onto a track and turn right. At the end of the track there are two field gates in quick succession to pass through and out onto a road.

Cross the road diagonally to the right to a stone squeeze stile. From it, drop down the footpath for Woodwell. Follow the path along, passing to the right of a square, enclosed pond, which is close to where the water comes out of the limestone cliff face. Just ahead, the path comes up to the cliff face, which is climbed with care.

At the top of the cliff, turn left to go along the path through the woodland, close to the edge of the cliff for about 40 metres and then turning right to go over limestone rock. Turn left onto a main path at its end to go to a stile. (For those not wishing to go over the cliff, go through the squeeze stile from the road and take the path to the right, pass above the cliff face and come to the stile.)

Follow the grassy path round to the right, going to an upper level of the field, where turn left. Go over a stile in a fence and follow the path through woodland. After passing through a squeeze stile, the path turns right to go along by the boundary wall of a house. As the path is followed, it becomes a proper lane and then comes out onto a road where turn right. In about thirty metres, turn left along a roadway, a signpost showing it is a footpath to the church. Go through a gateway and then straight ahead along the path, the tarred roadway going to the right, and enter a field. Go across the field by the wall on the left.

At the end of the field, come out onto a track and go straight ahead, crossing another track, and pass by a wall on the left; the church is on the other side of it. Come out onto a road where turn right for a few metres and then turn left along a path between two houses for Cove Road. On reaching the road, turn right and pass straight along it, going to the left of the Methodist church and to the main road.

Go a few metres along the main road to where there is a track to the left and by it is a wooden gateway leading to the path which runs up between the track and a field. The path goes into the woodland above and then finishes at a main track. Here, either turn left if not wanting to go to the Pepper Pot or otherwise turn right.

For the Pepper Pot, it is only a few metres to the right before another track is reached and there turn left, it being waymarked. (The waymarkers are for a circular route through the woodland, the whole of which takes about two hours to do.) Follow this track upwards, come to a junction and take the track

WALK 12

to the right and continue along it as it goes upwards and turns to the left. The track comes to a fork where take the left-hand path and keep following this main path, ignoring others both to the left and to the right. A gap in a wall is passed through and near it another waymarker shows that the path going up the hillside to the left is taken. This comes out at the viewpoint at the Pepper Pot, a monument commemorating Queen Victoria's Golden Jubilee in 1887. Return by the same route, remembering to cross over a path to the right on leaving the summit stretch so as to reach the main one again.

On arriving back at the track at the beginning of the diversion to the Pepper Pot, turn right and pass the way up from Silverdale. Shortly, the track passes along with a wall on the left. Two other paths to the right are passed, both of which can lead to the Pepper Pot. On reaching a roadway, turn right for Arnside Tower.

Follow the roadway past some houses and, at its end, continue along the path straight ahead at the edge of a garden and then through a stile in a wall into woodland.

The path through the woodland is a good one, passing through another gap in a wall and then goes along with a caravan site to the left. On reaching a fork in the path, take the one to the right, away from the caravans. Pass through some coppiced woodland and see Arnside Knott over to the left.

Come to an open area at the end of the track, and where there may be piles of soil, chippings, etc., go straight along the right-hand side and onto the grassy path going ahead, ignoring the one going to the right. At a fork, take the path to the right, quite close to a wall on the right, and see Arnside Tower ahead.

Arnside Tower was built close to the old agricultural and fishing community at Far Arnside, which was originally referred to as Heathwaite. The Tower, said to have been built around 1375, would provide protection against Scottish raids. It was burned in October 1602 and subsequently rebuilt. In 1884 a hurricane blew down the south-west angle.

Arnside lay in the parish of Beetham, and it was to that church that bodies were taken for burial. It did not become an ecclesiastical parish until 1870 and a civil parish until 1897. In 1770 the Rev William Hutton wrote that 'This very remote Corner of the Parish separated from it by Moss and Morass Ground is nevertheless within the great Liberty of Beetham'.

A number of large houses, such as 'Wood Close' and what is now the Albion Hotel were built in the early 1800's on the north side of Arnside Knott. Other properties, such as 'Ashmeadow' were considerably enlarged. It was originally an inn that had been converted into a Georgian dwelling, which had been built around it. Later, it became Earnseat School.

The main changes to Arnside followed on from the coming of the railway. For the first two years of the railway Arnside did not have a station; it was opened in 1859. However, from then on the village developed owing to easy access to Kendal, Lancaster and Barrow. The Crossfield brothers built many of the Victorian and Edwardian houses in the village.

The railway company built the pier in 1857 to compensate for the loss of Sandside as a port. It replaced an earlier and much smaller wooden pier close by. There was no promenade until 1897.

BWM12 Arnside viaduct from Arnside Knott.

Arnside became well-known for the Crossfield family's boatyard and, in total, they built around 1000 boats at this and other sites. Some were just rowing boats, but there were also various fishing vessels. The yard finally closed around 1951.

At the bottom of the path, close by the Tower ruins, there is a signpost and a ladder stile into the field where it stands. In the field, cross over to a track and follow it down to Arnside Tower Farm. At the end, go through the farmyard to the left of the farmhouse (18) and follow the farm roadway up to its top at a road.

WALK 12

Cross the road and go into the woodland in front. A National Trust signboard shows that Arnside Knott is being entered by Shilla Slopes. Go along the track, through a large wooden gate, by which there is a path to the right that is ignored, and continue on to where there is another track to the right, it going through a gate at its beginning. Follow that path, Hollins Path, along up the hillside with good views of parts of Morecambe Bay and around.

At the top of the path, turn left onto the main track in front and follow it along, passing a path coming up from the left (19). Go through a gateway and just in front is a Toposcope and viewpoint, with more good views of the Bay. From there, drop straight down the stony path in front to a roadway, where turn right.

The roadway becomes tarred and then comes to a junction. There, on the right, is a wooden kissing gate leading onto the path for Redhills Road. The path comes out a junction, where go straight ahead and come out onto Silverdale Road, where turn left down to Arnside promenade.

Turn right along the promenade, pass the shops and the pier and, perhaps, walk by the shore to the car park by the railway. Turn right along the road for the station just ahead.

16. Walk 12 goes ahead along the shore.
18. Walk 16 goes to the right, in front of the farm.
19. Walk 16 comes up this path and crosses here.

MORECAMBE BAY RAMBLES

WALK 13, SILVERDALE TO ARNSIDE VIA THE COAST

Easy.
6 miles, 9½ km.
Allow 3 hours.

A mainly coastal walk.

From Silverdale station, turn left and follow the road for about a third of a mile to where it splits for Carnforth and for Silverdale village. Go straight up the road to the right for about a mile to where there is a junction for the centre of the village, where there are bus stops. If not wanting to look round the village, go straight past the junction, round to the left, and then turn down Shore Road to (15) the shore. On reaching it, turn right along the beach, providing that the tide is not too high. As a broad open area on the right is reached, the cave at the Cove is seen in the rock cliff ahead. Go up this open area and onto the road at the top.

Follow the road to a junction, where turn left along the Arnside road. It is followed for about 250 metres and, as it turns left, follow the path to the right, its being for Far Arnside. Go through a metal gate into a caravan site and then, as the first caravan is reached, turn left along the footpath and cross the roadway and then straight across a grassy area to another roadway, where turn right. A few metres along the roadway a waymarker indicates the path going off to the left, which is followed.

The path goes over a part of a field to a small metal gate to pass through and straight across the next field to a wooden kissing gate. From it, follow the wall on the right to reach the road left earlier at a large kissing gate. Cross the road and continue straight ahead along the minor road for Far Arnside, passing a path for Arnside Knott.

Pass through the holiday park and come to a junction, where take the left-hand path down to the shore. Walk along the shingle of the shore and on coming to a rocky outcrop to the right there is the beginning of a path going along at the edge of the woodland. (If going too far along the shore and missing the beginning of the path, it can be seen and joined just above the shore.) Follow the main path along through the woodland, which is old coppicing, with the shore down to the left.

The path goes up a bit and is close to the edge of a cliff; it can be a bit rough in places. With White Creek to be seen in front, the path turns inland from the coast. Pass another path coming in from the right and continue along,

WALK 13

circling round towards another caravan park. The path comes out onto a track by the park, where turn right to follow it along and come out onto the coast again at New Barns. Keep on along the track going round to the right and along the roadway at the head of the shore.

BWM13 Arnside, the beach at New Barn.

The path to follow then leaves the roadway (16) and goes left following the shoreline for a short distance to a path that bears right into woodland. Go over a stile into a field and then straight along it with the Bay on the left and woodland on the right. At the end of the field there is a stile leading down onto the beach and, from it, turn right for Arnside. Go along the shore, the way followed somewhat depending on the tide, and come to a concrete promenade to follow into Arnside. (Alternatively, follow the shore all the way from Newbarns, tide permitting.) This promenade comes out onto a road and promenade, which is followed round, passing by the shops etc., the pier, and round to the railway station. There are bus stops on the way. The former station buildings are now the base of the *Arnside and Silverdale Area of Outstanding Natural Beauty*, the walks between the rivers Keer and Kent passing through parts of the area.

15. Walk 10 can be used to here instead.
16. Walk 16 goes up the roadway.

MORECAMBE BAY RAMBLES

WALK 14, SILVERDALE TO ARNSIDE VIA HAWES WATER

Easy.
4¼ miles, 6¾ km.
Allow two hours.

Visit marshland, woodland and farmland and a less frequently visited part of Arnside.

Turn right along the road on leaving the station and on reaching the first house on the right there is a wooden stile into a field, a signpost indicating it is the path for Leighton Moss. Cross the stile and go down the field towards a white gate leading onto the railway line. Cross the line with care. At the far side, cross the stone step stile and follow the path to the entrance to Trowbarrow. Turn left along the track to the road just ahead and then go to the right along it. (The road can be used all the way going a few metres further from the station and then turning right.)

On coming to the end of the road, continue straight ahead into what is part of the Gaitbarrow Nature Reserve, and is woodland. Come to stile on the right, at the corner of a wall and fencing, and cross it to follow the path round to the left and then by a wall on the right. (Before crossing the stile, a short diversion can be taken to Hawes Water by continuing straight ahead, and there is a permissive path that can be followed from there.) Ignore the kissing gate and path to the right, but continue ahead along the path, which then bears round more to the left. There is a walkway over some marshy ground, at the far end of which is the other end of the permissive path.

Continue along the path, catching glimpses of Hawes Water on the way. (At one point there is a short and obvious diversion which can be taken to where the water can be seen.) Pass along by a wall with an open area on the left and at the head of that area there is a junction of paths, one going off to the right, which is the one to be taken. It is quite a luxuriant area for growth, with limestone to the right.

A stile leads out onto a road, which is crossed, and then pass over another stile onto a track followed through woodland. Cross a wooden stile by a field gate and then follow the grassy track to another stile by a field gate ahead, passing a very good specimen ash tree.

The way now mainly used is to go just to the right of the track that had been followed and then along the field with the wall of the track just over on the left. At the end of that stretch there is a little stone bridge to cross to a stile.

WALK 14

Once over it, the grassy path bears left across the field. It is an area with a lot of bird life around to be heard and seen. Cross over another bridge, made of stone slabs, and then go along the field bearing towards the right to the trees on the far side of a wall in front. Go towards a corner in the field where there is a large metal field gate and to its right a stone step stile through the wall. Follow the grassy track straight across the field towards a metal field gate that can be seen. By it there is a stone stile out onto the road.

BWM14 Stone slab bridge over Leighton Beck.

Turn left along the road and pass two junctions to the right. Just past the second junction there is a small wooden gateway leading into a field on the left. Go over the field bearing right towards Hagg Wood seen ahead. As you go along the path there is a line of rather higher ground caused by a line of rock on the right. At a dip in it, turn right to follow the path through and then join a major track coming from the road, and turn left along it.

MORECAMBE BAY RAMBLES

Continue along the track to the railway, pass under the railway line and then come to a large metal field gate and, there, immediately turn right by a signpost for Arnside Station and Black Dyke (20). The path goes along by the railway line, crossing a wooden stile on the way, and enters a field through a metal field gate and passes across to a stile by another metal field gate a few metres ahead. It leads onto a small lane by some farm buildings a little to the left. Follow the lane, at the end of which there is another path to the left for the Silverdale Road. (Alternatively, turning right to the road and then turning left reach Arnside station reached in about half a mile.)

Go straight up the path at the edge of woodland, with houses and gardens on the right. The path comes out onto a private road and by the first of the houses at its end turns left to go along the edge of their garden and out onto another road. There, continue straight ahead, going slightly upwards, for Silverdale Road, where turn right for Arnside.

Where another road comes up from below on the right, adjacent to Our Lady of Lourdes Catholic Church, there is a bridleway on the right, dropping down towards the station. Follow the bridleway down to come out onto a road and there turn left for about 150 metres for the station.

This walk and the next walk can easily be linked together to make a circular trip.

20. Walk 16 comes under the railway bridge.
21. Walk 16 goes straight to the station.

WALK 15

WALK 15, ARNSIDE, LEIGHTON, SILVERDALE

Easy.
6¼ miles, 10 km.
Allow 2½ to 3 hours.

Visit a former Pele Tower, an old industrial site and a nature reserve.

This walk and the previous walk can easily be linked together to make a circular trip.

Turn left along the road from Arnside station and follow it for just under half a mile to a crossroads, the road to the right being for Silverdale and the one to the left being a tarred roadway past some houses, which are at the end of a field on the left. Turn left, there is a signpost for Kirkby Lonsdale twelve miles distant, and pass the houses. At the end of the roadway, cross the railway track with care and then follow the path straight along between two fences. It comes out into a field and there take the grassy path straight ahead, its being of doubtful visibility, passing over reclamation land.

Assuming you have got the line across the field right, come to a wooden kissing gate into the next field and then continue along the grassy path ahead from there. Pass a little waymarker showing you bear a little to the left and at the end of the field there are steps out onto a road. Cross the road and through a squeeze stile opposite. Go up a limestone outcrop at the top of which there is a stile into the field in front. Once through it, turn left for a few metres to the next stile to pass through. From there, cross the field to the good track serving the caravan site and go down it to its end. Pass through a squeeze stile to the right of a field gate and out onto a road where turn right towards Hazelslack Tower Farm.

Pass the farm and at the road junction ahead turn right (22). In about 100 metres, as the road bears to the right, go straight ahead along the bridleway. It is followed for just under a quarter of a mile to the end of some trees on the right across a narrow field on the right. There, the track turns to the left and straight ahead there is a field gate to go through. Cross straight over the field, aiming to the right of an ash tree, to come to a small wooden bridge spanning Leighton Beck. Cross it and then turn left to go across the field to a stile by an open gateway in a wall.

From there, go along by the wall on the right to the gateway in front. The following field is crossed a little over to the right towards a gateway in a wall

MORECAMBE BAY RAMBLES

and the way is a little higher up the slope. Cross the next field by the wall on the right and then pass through another gateway to follow the well-used farm track along. Here it passes the site of the former Leighton Furnace with Leighton Beck below to the left. At a metal field gate, come out onto a road and turn left.

Very little is known about Hazelslack Tower. There is a legend that it was built around 1375, but this is thought to be unlikely. It is built of limestone rubble and is about 42 feet to the top of the battlements. It was in ruins by 1811.

Leighton Furnace was an ironworks erected by the Furness proprietors of ironworks. It was probably built at the end of 1705 or early in 1706, but could have been around 1713. Ore was brought across Morecambe Bay from Stainton in Furness, but there is also a lease dated 1719 which refers to mines

BWM15 Site of Leighton Furnace.

of lead, copper, iron and tin in the wastes of the Manor of Yealand. It is probable that the furnace was erected owing to the scarcity of wood, for the vital charcoal, in Furness. It was built against the side of a hill by Leighton Beck, needed for its water supply. The bellows were operated by a very large overshot waterwheel. An explosion damaged the furnace in 1806, resulting in its closure. Now, only its site remains visible.

Follow the road to the next junction by which there is a squeeze stile on the right leading into a field. Go up the field, bearing a little to the left, away from the wall, and come to a gap in the hedge-line. From it, there is an indicator, bear a little further to the right towards some trees in front. Turn right into the trees and come to a stile in a fence, cross it and then turn left to cross another stile in a wall into the following field where bear a little to the right over the field. Pass another indicator, and gradually approach the wall over to the right, on the far side of which is Gait Barrows Nature Reserve, an area well worth a visit on its own.

Strictly, the right of way is by the wall, but people follow the grassy path a little to its left to go to a squeeze stile in the wall in front and to the left of the corner of the field. Go ahead from that stile, bearing towards the far right corner of the field where there is a stile to cross. From it, turn right onto the earthen path and follow it along, its winding a little on the way. Ignore a path going to the left.

Come to another wooden stile to cross and follow the path through the trees to a stile leading out onto a track. Turn left along the track and at the junction ahead turn right to go through the field gate and onto a broad gravel track. Follow this track along through a field gate, which is by a permissive way leading down to Storrs Lane, the road for Silverdale station. From the field gate, continue along the track to its end at another gate, by which there is a good view to Leighton Moss, and out onto Storrs Lane. Turn left along the road for about a hundred metres to where there are steps to the right, leading through a wall. From them, pass in front of the dwellings and come to a field gate to pass through.

Follow the track along as it bends to the right and then fades as it approaches a wall. Turn left to go along by the wall, which is shortly replaced by a hedge. Pass through a field gate and follow the track along the wall on the right to come to a metal kissing gate. It is a very clear farm track which is followed through to Leighton Hall Home Farm.

On coming out onto the roadway (17), turn right and follow it down, passing Grisedale Farm on the way to a field gate into another field. In that field, the track splits and the one to the right is followed down to the field gate leading onto the Causeway across Leighton Moss. Cross straight over The Causeway, where there is a public hide for observing, birds, and come out onto Storrs Lane again, where turn left. Go straight up the road and pass the RSPB centre at Myers Farm on the way to the road junction in front. There, turn right for Silverdale station.

Refreshments can be obtained at the RSPB centre and for a charge to non-members other hides can be visited. Who knows, you may hear a bittern boom and even be very lucky and see one.

17. Walk 11 is joined here.
22. Walk 17 also uses this route to here.

WALK 16

WALK 16, ARNSIDE, ARNSIDE KNOTT, ARNSIDE TOWER, ARNSIDE

Generally easy, depending on the shore and tide.
5¼ miles, 8½ km.
Allow 2½ hours.

This is a delightful walk that can be done as a whole or linked and done in part with another walk. It is very good for seeing birds and plant life.

From Arnside station entrance, turn right along the road to pass by the shops and the pier. At the Fountain, drop down onto the beach and go along at the head of it. Either continue along the beach or go up to the shortly reached concrete promenade above it. Pass the end of a roadway to a house and continue along the shingle or sand, depending on the state of the tide. Pass the yacht club with its slipway and, at its end, go up to the left to the field above. Cross the wooden stile into the field and turn right to follow the path by the fence just above the shore.

BWM16 Morecambe Bay from Arnside Knott.

MORECAMBE BAY RAMBLES

At the end of the field there is a field gate and just to its left there is a wooden stile to cross. Follow the path along at the edge of woodland and then drop down to the head of the beach again (22). Go along the path to a roadway where turn left. As the roadway makes a 'U' turn round to the left, there is a metal kissing gate on the right by a signpost for Arnside and Silverdale. Go straight along the path and into Copridding Wood.

Follow the path up the hill ahead, ignoring two paths to the left, and come to a wall with a large wooden gate in it, and by that a small one for pedestrians. Continue along this main path, over a rather more open area, ignoring a path to the left and another crossing over and come to a wall. Turn left to go along by the wall and in about 100 metres come to a public bridleway for Heathwaite and Arnside Tower. Turn right onto the bridleway, going through a wooden gate.

Just after leaving the gate there is a gravel path going uphill to the left to follow. There are views back to Silverdale and across the Bay to Grange from this path. At a crossroads of paths keep on going straight ahead up the path in front. On coming to paths to the left and the right in quick succession (19) go straight ahead higher up the Knott. At the next fork, follow the gravel path to the left, passing the remains of knotted trees (the right-hand path leads to the triangulation pillar at the actual summit of the Knott), and pass a memorial seat. On reaching a wall, turn right, do not pass through the kissing gate, and follow the path as it drops down. It leaves the wall and then comes to another one, at the end of which go out onto the road and turn right.

In about a quarter of a mile, turn down the roadway to the left (18) for Arnside Tower Farm. Pass through the farmyard and then by the house. In the field then entered, immediately turn left. Go straight along the field, passing below Arnside Tower ruins and at the far side there is a wooden field gate into the woodland in front. Ignore the metal field gate a few metres to its left.

Follow the path through Middlebarrow Wood and come to another track where turn left, a signpost indicating that it is for Black Dyke. Go straight along the field by the fence on the right, close to the railway line. At the end of the field a wooden footbridge crosses a drainage dyke and leads into the next field, which is crossed in the same way. At its end there is a concrete farm track, which comes from under the railway (20). This is crossed to go straight ahead to a stile in front.

WALK 16

Cross another wooden stile and bear diagonally left to go between the new farm buildings in front. At the end of them, go over a stone stile onto a lane and at its end (21) turn right onto the road. There, turn left for Arnside station (23) about half a mile distant.

18. Walk 12 comes up this roadway and onto the Knott at the right.
19. Walk 12 crosses here.
20. Walk 14 is joined here.
21. Walk 14 goes up the Silverdale road.
22. Alternatively, as with walk 13 but in reverse, assuming the tide is right, follow the shore to here.
23. The path for Hazelslack used in walks 15 and 17 is passed on the right at the junction with the Silverdale road.

MORECAMBE BAY RAMBLES

WALK 17, ARNSIDE, HAZELSLACK, FAIRY STEPS, SANDSIDE, ARNSIDE

Easy, but limestone rock can be slippery when wet.
6½ miles, 9½ km. Excluding the diversion.
Allow 4 hours plus about 35 minutes for the diversion.

A limestone walk passing a pele tower, over the famous Fairy Steps and down to the shore.

Turn left along the road from Arnside station and follow it for just under half a mile to a crossroads, the road to the right being for Silverdale and the one to the left being a tarred roadway past some houses, which are at the end of a field on the left. Turn left, there is a signpost for Kirkby Lonsdale twelve miles distant, and pass the houses. At the end of the roadway, cross the railway track with care and then follow the path straight along between two fences. It comes out into a field and there take the grassy path straight ahead, its being of doubtful visibility, passing over reclamation land.

Assuming you have got the line across the field right, come to a wooden kissing gate into the next field and then continue along the grassy path ahead from there. Pass a little waymarker showing you bear a little to the left and at the end of the field there are steps out onto a road. Cross the road and through a squeeze stile opposite. Go up a limestone outcrop at the top of which there is a stile in the field in front. Once through it, turn left for a few metres to the next stile to pass through. From there, cross the field to the good track serving a caravan site and go down it to its end. Pass through a squeeze stile to the right of a field gate and out onto a road where turn right towards Hazelslack Tower Farm.

Pass the farm and follow the road the road to its end, cross the road in front (22) and just to the left of a field gate there is a stone slab stile leading into a field. Go straight up the field by the wall on the right, into another field by another stone slab stile, and continue up by the wall again. At the top of the field there is a wooden field gate leading onto a track going straight ahead into the woodland. This limestone track is followed to a rock face where it turns left and then right to go up to the top between the rocks. This is not Fairy Steps, as some people have mistakenly thought.

From the top of the rocks, continue straight along the path and come to the rock face with Fairy Steps. Going up the steps can be avoided by taking the path to the left which comes to an indicator cairn mentioned later. It is much

WALK 17

more fun going up the narrow steps in a cleft in the cliff. Do it without touching the sides and legend has it that your wish will be granted.

Fairy Steps are on the old coffin route from Arnside to Beetham, which was the mother church. Coffins had to be raised up the cliff face by rope as they could not be carried up the steps. Another coffin route brought corpses over the Kent estuary from Witherslack, crossing over where Arnside Viaduct now stands.

BWM17 Hazelslack Tower and Farm.

At the top of the steps, go straight ahead into the woodland, there is a waymarker. The clear path comes to a crossroads of paths with a gate by them and there turn left. Follow this track along to come to the indicator cairn mentioned earlier. Here, the track divides, the one to the right being taken. It comes out onto a road where turn right and in a few metres there is a squeeze stile to the left, it is signposted for Sandside and Haverbrack. Go through it and take the right-hand path straight in front.

MORECAMBE BAY RAMBLES

Follow the path as it bears to the right and then goes ahead again. On reaching a fork, turn right and then come to a signpost at a junction of paths where take the one to the left for Hollins Well. The path is a very clear one. At some buildings it goes to the right and then looks out over the Bay.

On arriving at a wooden field gate leading into private land, turn left to go through a wooden kissing gate. Go down the field by the wall on the right, ignoring a gateway into another field. There are very good views of Morecambe Bay, across to Whitbarrow and round to Milnthorpe. At the end of the field a wooden kissing gate leads out onto a very minor road, which is crossed to the stile by the wall on the left.

Follow the path down by the wall. Enter some very narrow woodland and go along by the wall on the right. A wooden ladder stile takes the path over a wall and then continue for a few metres further to the main road between Arnside and Milnthorpe. If time is pressing, turn left here, otherwise the following loop can be done back to this point taking around forty minutes.

Turn right along the road for about a third of a mile and just before reaching the bridge over the River Bela (23) there is a wooden kissing gate in the wall on the left. There are also bus stops here. Go through it and then down the field with the Bela on the right. At the end there is a wooden stile leading out onto the foreshore, where turn left. Follow the path round at the head of the shore, by the fence on the left. Just after the end of the fence there is a slope up to the old railway line. At the top, continue to the right along the track of the old railway to its end at the road at the beginning of this loop.

Turn right for Sandside. Shortly, assuming that the tide is not too high, drop down to walk at the head of the shore, just below the road. Pass the *Ship Inn* and soon afterwards come up onto the road and follow the footpath by it.

At the end of the footpath, reached at a road junction, drop down to the head of the beach again, tide permitting. On coming to a fence, cross a stile and then turn up to the trackbed of the old railway line. Go straight along it and at its end come to a large wooden gate. Pass through it, along a short stretch of track and then turn left to the platforms of Arnside station.

Sandside was the port for Milnthorpe, and was often referred to as 'Milnthrop Sandside', but vessels beached at various points between Sandside and along the Bela to Milnthorpe. The village had a very imposing railway station for its size and the line, which ran between Arnside and Hincaster, was used for the transport of limestone from the quarry. Passenger traffic ceased in 1942 but the line continued for freight until 1963. A fine viaduct built of local limestone with red sandstone pediments and copings crossed the River Bela.

It had three open box girder arches. Sadly, 1966 saw its demolition.

This was the only sea-port in the old county of Westmorland, but was never of major importance as it had no stone quay, but there was a wharf at Dixies. The port had its own customs officer who saw that taxes had been paid on imported goods and Excise Duty was paid on the salt that was exported. The Custom House was in Park Road in Milnthorpe and it was a dependant port under Lancaster.

A ferry used to operate from Dixies Inn, the ferryman charging 3d at high tide and 6d at low tide for his services.

At one time there were ten pubs in the Sandside area and it was known for being sleazy.

22. Walk 15 also uses this route to here, but turns right along the road.
23. Walk 18 can be joined to Levens Bridge by crossing this bridge.

MORECAMBE BAY RAMBLES

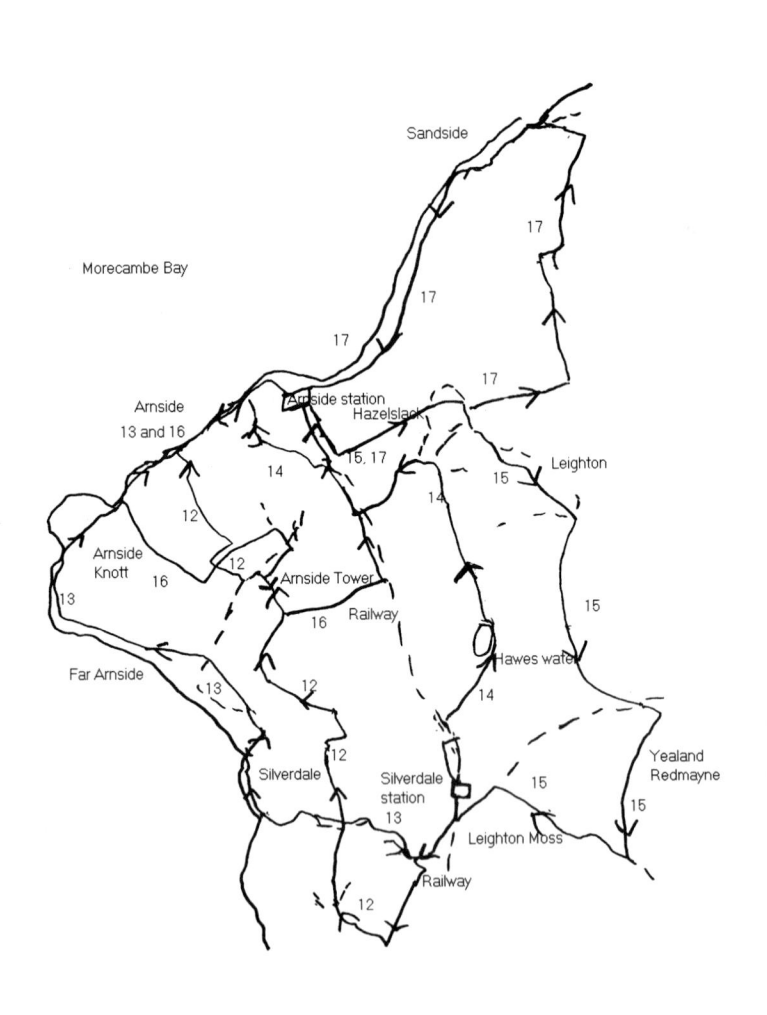

Bay walks 12, 13, 14, 15, 16 & 17

WALK 18

WALK 18, MILNTHORPE, COASTAL WAY, HEVERSHAM, LEVENS BRIDGE

Easy.
5 miles, 8km.
Allow 2¾ hours.

Pass over reclamation land and farm land and then through a plantation to Levens Hall.

Milnthorpe's name refers to a mill and a village. There is still a working mill where all manner of combs are manufactured. However, although it still has an internal waterwheel, it is now powered by electricity and not the River Bela. At one time there were about twenty mills.

It was not until 1837 that St Thomas' church was consecrated; prior to then Milnthorpe had been a joint township with Heversham. Even then, it was just a chapelry within the parish of Heversham until 1896.

There were a number of inns and beer houses in the village, including the Bull's Head on Beetham Road. On the coming of the turnpike road, which was authorised in 1818, no attempt was made to widen the gap between it and a row of cottages, leaving a gap of less than twelve feet for traffic.

A market is still held in the Square every Friday, where a wide range of goods and produce can be purchased. The original Charter was granted to the Manor of Heversham in 1334, when the market was held on a Wednesday. During the First World War the market nearly died, no weekly markets being held and only stalls selling surplus produce coming from time to time. Other traders visited and traded from the Market Cross, resulting in the market never completely dying out and the market rights lapsing. The Market Cross was the first building in Milnthorpe to be listed. It was also used for proclamations and there is a photograph from May 1910 showing the proclamation of King George V as Monarch.

Dallam Tower, standing in Dallam Park, was originally a pele tower. The Manor of Heversham was purchased by Edward Wilson of Nether Levens in 1614. Thomas Wilson, his step son-in-law, inherited his estates and his descendants moved into the tower in 1720, by which date it had newly been rebuilt. The porch of Tuscan columns and the side pavilions were added in around 1826.

MORECAMBE BAY RAMBLES

The road from Milnthorpe to Sandside used to run on the south side of the river until 1813, when the present road and bridge over the Bela were built. The old road bridge remains as a footbridge leading into Dallam Park. During the following years, the hamlet of Scout Bank on the northern bank of the river was cleared to improve the view for the Wilson family. At Dallam Wheel, where the river turns to flow north, there were ship building and timber yards.

From the bus stops at Milnthorpe, go past the Square and shops to the main road and cross at the crossing. Pass along the road in front, for Arnside, and continue along it to where a bridge on the left, the old road bridge, spans the River Bela. Cross it into Dallam Park, and there bear to the right in the direction of Dallam Tower. As the park is crossed, a metal kissing gate to the right of a large metal gate is seen in the fence in front, opposite the right hand end of Dallam Tower. Pass through it and turn right along the minor road to the main Arnside road where turn right for a few metres (23).

Cross Milnthorpe Bridge and immediately after there is a road to the left to be followed, it being a typical reclamation road. At Marsh Farm the tarred road turns right, part of the reclamation road continuing ahead. Turn right along the tarred road follow it across Milnthorpe Marsh, over a small bridge spanning the main drain, past Moss Side Farm and up to the busy A6 road. Cross the road and go straight up to Heversham church.

Reclamation roads cross former mosses which have been drained to provide agricultural land. Typically, the roads run in straight lines with right-angle bends. On either side of the surfaced roadway there is a broad grass verge and a ditch to drain off the water.

There was much land that was Common, Mosses or Waste Grounds in the Heversham and Levens area in the early 1800's. The Enclosure Acts of the time were to encourage farming by enclosing the lands and exonerating them from tithes. Through the patronage of the church, the Master, Fellows and Scholars of Trinity College, Cambridge were owners of some of the Commons rights and received some of the enclosed lands. The vicarage received 650 acres.

The name 'Heversham' dates from Anglian times, probably of the seventh century, but possibly the late sixth century. The "ham", meaning a farmstead, village or estate, would be founded by the Anglian Chief Haefar.

WALK 18

St Peter's Church dominates Heversham. Not only does it claim to be the oldest church in the former county of Westmorland, but it is one of the earliest Christian sites in Cumbria. It is probable that the first religious buildings on the site were of an early Anglian monastery, which would be a group of huts and a wall. The church has part of the shaft of an Anglian grave cross. The building has been much enlarged and altered from the original building of around 1100 AD. The tower, thought by Lancaster architect E G Paley to date back to the eleventh century, was rebuilt between 1869 and 1871. Its foundations had been weakened with the lowering of the ancient track by it on the construction of the turnpike road in 1823.

BWM04 St Peter's Church, Heversham.

Close to the path above the church stands the building of the 'Grammar School ', which was founded in 1613 by Edward Wilson of Nether Levens, an ancestor of the Dallam Tower Wilson family. The school was exclusively for boys, provision being made for two of whom, otherwise without the financial means, to continue with their education at universities. The school was replaced by a new building at the southern end of the village in 1878.

At the top of the road there are some steps leading into the churchyard and, once up them, turn left and then diagonally right across the grassy path over the churchyard, starting at the end of the church. That path joins another one, where turn left to go through a small iron gate and out of the churchyard. Go up a path crossing the field in front. Pass through a squeeze stile by a field gate and from it continue on ascending the next field. On reaching a metal kissing gate on the right, go through it and then bear right to pass the corner of the plantation in front.

As the grassy way up the field is followed, a cluster of trees comes into view on the right, turn towards them. There is a waymarker by the tress showing the path bears diagonally left and, from it, keep going to what has by then become the far left corner in front. There, a little wooden gate and some stone steps lead over the wall.

Cross straight over the next field by the grassy path in front. At the end of the field, just before a field gate coming out onto a farm track, there is a squeeze stile on the right to go through from where follow the path down, close to the wall on the right. At its end there is another stone squeeze stile leading out onto a road where turn left.

In about a quarter of a mile, come to Mabbin Hall on the right. There, follow the byway going straight past the dwelling and continue straight along it. Note a round mound to be seen on the right, in the plantation, shortly before reaching the A6, it being a former icehouse with the wood named after it. Turn right at the end of the track to go along the A6 to the bus stops by Levens Bridge close to Levens Hall. The one for the south is reached close to the bridge and the one for the north being across the bridge and a few metres along the Grange road to the left. Alternatively, turn left to go along the road and back into Leasgill and Heversham.

Levens Hall, by Levens Bridge, dates back to around 1250 to 1300 and is a fortified structure with a pele tower as well as a hall. It was sold to the Bellinghams in 1562 and it was they who converted it into an Elizabethan house. Alan Bellingham ran up gambling debts and it changed hands again in 1688 when Colonel James Grahme acquired the property, traditionally by the turn of the Ace of Hearts. It is believed that the heart motifs of some of the drainpipe brackets relates to that tradition.

The building has been much extended over the years, including the west wing by Colonel Grahme. Throughout the Hall is magnificent wooden panelling. Also, there are some very fine furnishings, particularly the walnut dining chairs in the dining room.

Colonel Grahme was out of favour in Court Society owing to having supported James II, who abdicated. He took with him to Levens Monsieur Guillaume Beaumont, who had been gardener to the former king and was similarly out of favour. Beaumont set to work on the grounds around the Hall and laying out Levens Park, with its famous avenue of oak trees.

WALK 18

The first feature he created in the grounds of the Hall was the Ha-Ha, which gives the impression of an open vista, but on approaching its edge it can be seen that there is a barricade to prevent sheep and cattle from entering the gardens. It is the first one recorded in Britain.

The topiary garden is what makes Levens Hall unique; it is the best and most extensive in the world. Some of the trees and bushes are over 300 years old, and have been cut to a wide variety of designs. They include Great Umbrellas, Peacocks, Chess Pieces and the fascinating Judge's Wig amongst many others.

Maintaining the hedges and the topiary is an enormous task, the Great Beech Hedge alone is 500 yards long. It takes two people six weeks to trim the Beech Hedge and takes two months to trim the topiary each year.

Tucked away in a corner using the wall by the A6 road on one side, is a small triangular building. This is the Smoke House to which seventeenth century smokers were banished, and it is as far from the Hall as possible.

Mannex & Co Directory of 1851 says that "Amid these sylvan scenes the mayor and corporation of Kendal, with the friends of the successive lords of Levens, have, since the days of Colonel Graham, spent many a jovial evening, after proclaiming the fair at Milnthorp, on the 12th of May."

23. By turning left to go by the Bela, walk 17 is joined.

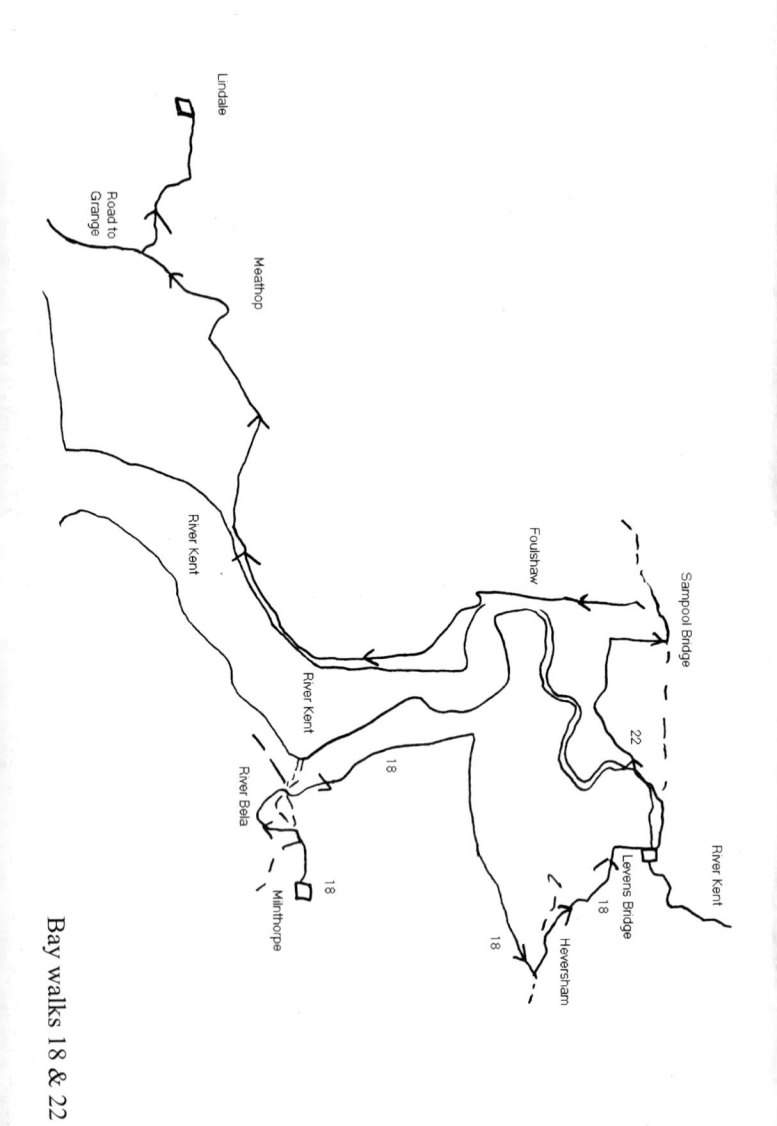

MORECAMBE BAY RAMBLES

BWC01 passing through sea lock, Glasson.
BWC02 Boats moored at Morecambe.

BWC03 Morcambe Bay sunset at Bolton-le-Sands.
BWC04 'Alec and Laura' with visitors, Carnforth Station.

BWC05 Black-headed gull at nest, Leighton Moss.
BWC06 Arnside Pier.

BWC07 Kent estuary, Sandside.
BWC08 Fountain and Levens Hall.

WALK 19

WALK 19, LEVENS BRIDGE, BRIGSTEER, WHITBARROW, LEVENS BRIDGE

Easy
12¼ miles, 19½ km.
Allow 6 hours.

A pleasant walk over reclamation land, farmland and through woodland.

What is now known as Levens Village was formerly called Beathwaite Green. The "thwaite" element of the name shows that in Viking times this was a clearing in a woody area all around. The Domesday Book of 1086 records the area as 'Lefuenes'. The parish of Levens included Beathwaite Green, part of Leasgill to the south, and part of Brigsteer.

The church, a chapelry in the parish of Heversham, was built in 1828 at a cost of £2,000, which was a gift by the Hon and Mrs F G Howard of Levens Hall, as was a commodious house for the clergyman.

If coming from the north, leave the bus at Levens Bridge, cross the A6 and onto the Grange road. Go past the bus stop close to Levens Hall and, at the road junction, cross over and go up the road on the right to the next junction, where go ahead for Levens Village. Coming from the south, leave the bus at the stop before the flyover, (and very shortly after leaving Levens Bridge) and walk back the few yards to the road to the right leading to Levens Village.

Walk up the road to Levens, pass the shop and come to a road junction. Go left across it, ignoring the road for Brigsteer and then over the crossroads a few metres ahead by the Methodist Church. Follow the road ahead for about half a mile, with views across the bottom of the Lyth Valley on the left.

Pass Quaggs Farm and a letter box on the left and then about 100 metres beyond, at the end of Inglewood Barn, turn left onto a track which goes to the right in a few metres for the track that is the footpath to Park End. Follow the track along to where it turns left and there is a kissing gate by a field gate straight ahead. Go through it and follow the track along through the wood. At its end, come out into a field and bear right up it going to the far right corner by the farm and out onto the road there, where turn left.

At the road junction at the beginning of Brigsteer village you can go left or right, the road to the right passing the *Wheatsheaf Inn* (where turn left), the one to the left being lower. The roads meet up again and a few metres beyond there is a turning to the left for the Lyth Valley. Turn down the road and onto the Moss.

MORECAMBE BAY RAMBLES

Brigsteer was spelt 'Bryggstere' in 1227, its first recorded mention. It is suggested that the name refers to a Bullock and a bridge. Jeffrey's Map of 1770 shows the village as just one street with a road leading off to Kendal. Below were the moss lands that form part of the Lyth Valley and which are mentioned in the Enclosure Act for the Heversham area. There is no road shown across the valley, it coming after the enclosures and draining the very level area below the village.

BWM19 Brigsteer.

The road turns left at the far end of the Moss, where turn right onto the untarred roadway by the farm. (There is no right of way over Lyth Moss Roads, which are used at own risk. The alternative is to continue along the road to the next junction and turn right for The Row.) Where the roadway forks, turn left. In a few hundred metres there is a track to the left, its crossing a bridge at the junction. Follow that track up to the main road, where turn right. In about a hundred metres take a road to the left for The Row. On reaching the houses the road turns right. At the first bend, the path to follow leaves the road and goes through a gateway. Follow the path round between the houses and it then becomes a farm track between two hedges.

WALK 19

A stile by a field gate is crossed at its end and in the field immediately turn right to follow another stretch of track between hedges and then walls. Follow the path along from there, going upwards. As it comes into the open near an old gateway, turn left along the top of the field to a stile by a field gate in the top left corner. Cross into a damson plantation for a few metres, following a grassy path going over to the left. A wooden stile is crossed, leading to a stone squeeze stile just ahead.

The stile leads into some woodland where follow the path going diagonally to the right. Pass a much less used path on the left and in another 100 metres or so the path joins a good track, where turn left. Follow it along amongst the trees and bracken and come to a diagonal crossroads of forestry tracks, which is passed straight over to the track in front.

Pass through a gateway at a very broad stone stile in a wall and continue ahead. Pass a waymarked path going left for Gilbirks (24) and a few metres ahead pass a waymarked track to the right (but the marker may not be clearly seen for surrounding growth). Continue on ahead, ignoring another track joining on the right.

At the next junction, where another forestry track joins from the left, turn to the right, that being the track to follow. A few metres further on another forestry track crosses, but continue ahead past the waymarker. From there, it is quite a distance to the next junction with a forestry road, where turn right.

The track passes through a gap in a wall and comes to a junction of tracks about 15 metres beyond, where turn left into the trees. Drop down the track and come to a stile across it, just before reaching a farm.

Pass part of the farm buildings and then turn right to follow the track along. It goes under White Scar, which towers above. After leaving the Scar the track becomes a tarred roadway and then turns left. It joins the old main road coming from the left. A gate to the right of a cattle grid is passed through out onto the busy modern main road, where turn left to go along the verge.

Before the present A590 road was built in the 1970's, the rather narrow and bendy road was part of the main A590. It is on the site of the turnpike road of 1818. Anciently, there was a corduroy road made of logs lower than Sampool Bridge. Before the turnpike was built, the River Gilpin, which then followed its natural course, was crossed about 100 metres further upstream at Lythpool Bridge. Much of the road, where it crosses mosses, was floated on juniper cut from Whitbarrow Fell.

MORECAMBE BAY RAMBLES

In about half a mile there is a road junction where turn left and then pass Gilpin Bridge Inn and over Sampool Bridge by the footway on its left. At the end of the bridge there is a footpath to the left, by a house, which is followed over a stile and onto the reclamation embankment by the River Gilpin. Two stiles are crossed on the way to a stile leading out onto a minor road, where turn left for Levens village. Ignore a road going to the left on the way to the village and on coming out by the *Hare and Hounds* turn right. A few metres ahead there is another junction where turn left and go up the road.

There are some seats nearly opposite Levens church. Turn right by them to follow the footpath for Nether Levens, it passing through a wall and into a field at the end of a little cul de sac. Drop straight down the field towards a footbridge, which can be seen cross the A590, at its end. A wooden stile comes out onto a roadway close by the bridge, which is crossed. Follow the concrete roadway round past the farm and through a field gate out onto a road, where turn left.

This road comes out onto another road where turn right. Shortly, there is a stile in the hedge leading onto a permissive path at the edge of the field. At the end of the path a wooden stile is crossed and then turn right onto the riverside path and follow it through the woodland to its end close by Levens Bridge and the bus stops.

24. Walk 20 goes down this path.

WALK 20

WALK 20, LEVENS BRIDGE, WHITBARROW, LEVENS BRIDGE

Moderate.
12½ miles 20 km.
Allow 6½ hours.

This walk is an attractive mix of woodland and limestone country.

The bus stop from the north is roughly opposite the entrance to Levens Hall whilst that from the south is across the bridge and round the corner on the Grange road or the one a little further on nearer the village can be used.

BWM20 Topiary, Levens Hall.

    The walk starts at a footpath close to the bridge and is by the road junction. Follow it along the riverbank, with Levens Hall across the water. Come out onto the Grange road, cross it, go left and then and take the turning to the right for Levens Village. Go under the by-pass on what was part of the roadway before the road up above was built. At the junction, cross straight over, and continue along the road into Levens Village. The alternative bus stop from the south is by this junction.

MORECAMBE BAY RAMBLES

On entering the village turn left along Church Road and follow it along to its end where turn right. By the Hare and Hounds, a few metres away, turn left along another road for about a hundred metres and then turn left again, crossing a bridge and onto a reclamation road.

Follow the road along, with Whitbarrow straight in front. At a bend to the left, cross a stile on the right and then turn left along the embankment by the River Gilpin. As the path ends, by some houses, turn right to cross the footbridge by Sampool Bridge and then cross the Windermere road and continue straight along the road to the busy main road for Barrow, where turn right.

Go along the verge for about a quarter of a mile and, just after crossing a bridge, turn right onto the old road, go through a gate by the cattle grid and continue to a junction where take the roadway on the right. Just before reaching Raven's Lodge, the farm in front, turn left onto the bridleway into the woodland, passing through a field gate. Follow this good track along, come to some of the houses of Witherslack, pass a path dropping down to the left (25) and then about forty metres further on a permissive path leading off to the right (26). At a junction about two hundred metres ahead, take the path to the right, for Beck Head.

Climb over a stone step stile leading into a field and there drop down by the wall on the left to reach a field gate at the end. From it, go along the gravelled driveway, past some dwellings and come out onto a minor road where turn right. Continue ahead on reaching the end of the tarred road, passing some farm buildings, it being a bridleway.

The bridleway comes out onto a road where turn right. On reaching the entrance to Witherslack Hall School, turn right to go down the farm track (27) and through a wooden kissing gate which touches round limestone walling instead of the usual wood. Bear left along the path over the field, ignoring a permissive path on the left. Pass by a football field and at its end cross a wooden stile to go behind the goal.

From there, go along the earthen path into the woodland at a gap in the wall and turn left to come to a junction where turn right to go up the hillside. Just after the junction the path starts its ascent of the limestone up Whitbarrow Scar and this is quite steep. At the top, come to a limestone wall, pass through a gap in it and over a wooden stile to enter the Harvey Nature Reserve.

Follow the path upwards, with views over the Winster valley. The path leaves an area of silver birches and goes right, passing small limestone cairns indicating the way. It is a rather gravelly limestone path through limestone country as it makes its way to the memorial cairn, Lord's Seat (28), at the top

WALK 20

of Whitbarrow, where there are good views around and over to Morecambe Bay.

Whitbarrow is important both geologically for its limestone and as a nature reserve, particularly for its birds and butterflies. It has a number of paths over it, both rights of way and permitted paths. The name, meaning "The White Hill" comes from the Viking settlers. In 1898 a Viking sword was found at the foot of the Scar. Between the bottom of the valley at Witherslack and the 215 metre summit there are five of the six types of Carboniferous Limestone of South Lakeland. The most extensive one to be seen is the summit area of Urswick limestone. The occasional Silurian Grit erratic is to be seen on Whitbarrow, it having been brought by glaciers from the Lake District mountains. It will be noticed that the lichens growing on these rocks are different from those on the ones of limestone.

Following the Heversham enclosures, Whitbarrow was divided into Allotments. Flodder Allotment now forms the Harvey Nature Reserve. There is some grazing done as part of the management to keep scrub under control.

From Lord's Seat, turn left to follow the path, which very shortly bears right and starts to drop down towards a limestone cliff face. As it reaches the cliff, the path turns left and then comes to a wall with a stone step stile in it. Cross the stile and out of the Nature Reserve.

As the path through the fairly open woodland in front is followed, look out for a path dropping down to the left in about two hundred metres. It is easily missed if looking at a bird or butterfly or talking to a companion. Drop down the path, pass another coming down from the left, and come to a junction where turn left. In a few metres there is a path dropping down to the right, it is waymarked (24), going via Gilbirks. (If the path down to here has been missed, another one is reached after about 300 metres, there turn left, pass the end of the path that should have been descended, and come to the junction for Gilbirks.)

Drop down the Gilbirks path passing through woodland and then go up again a short distance before descending towards farmland in front. Cross a stile in a wall and bear to the left. Keep bearing left down the field to another waymarker by the end of the trees. There, turn left and cross over this narrow section of field to go through a field gate, and continue along the woodland path in front.

The path turns left and then goes upwards as it becomes a track, joining another where turn right. Buildings are to be seen through the trees on the

MORECAMBE BAY RAMBLES

right before the track comes out at a large limestone millstone, where turn right down an unsurfaced roadway. Pass some houses and come to a proper road where turn right. It is one with grass in the middle in places.

Pass down the road towards the River Gilpin and the reclaimed land below. Shortly after passing Draw Well there is a crossroads where turn right; this road is followed down to the main Lyth Valley road where turn right to Sampool Bridge.

Before the A5074 to the Lake District was constructed, the minor road used was the only way along this side of the Lyth Valley. The communities were each built round a source of fresh water and above the moss-lands down in the valley bottom.

Cross the bridge and at its end there is a footpath to the left, by a house. Follow it along and pass over a stile to the embankment by the river. Two stiles are crossed on the way to another leading out onto a minor road, where turn left for Levens village. Ignore a road going to the left and continue to the village, coming out by the *Hare and Hounds* where turn right. A few metres ahead there is another junction, where turn left and go up the road.

There are some seats nearly opposite Levens church. Turn right by them to follow the footpath for Nether Levens, it passing through a wall and into a field at the end of a little cul de sac. Drop straight down the field towards a footbridge, which can be seen cross the A590, at its end. A wooden stile comes out onto a roadway close by the bridge, which is crossed. Follow the concrete roadway round past the farm and through a field gate out onto a road, where turn left.

This road comes out onto another road where turn right. Shortly, there is a stile in the hedge leading onto a permissive path at the edge of the field. At the end of the path a wooden stile is crossed and then turn right onto the riverside path, used at the beginning of the walk, and follow it through the woodland to its end close by Levens Bridge and the bus stops.

24. Walk 19 follows the main path but goes to the right from the junction a few metres earlier.
25. Walk 21 comes up this path.
26. Walk 21 goes up the permissive path.
27. Walk 21 uses this path, but in the opposite direction, it turning left after coming along the farm track.
28. Walk 21 is met at the cairn.

WALK 21, WITHERSLACK, WHITBARROW, WITHERSLACK

Moderate.
7¼ miles, 11½ km.
Allow 4 hours.

Another mix of woodland and limestone walking.

Witherslack is a very straggly village passing up the valley from the A590. At the time of the enclosures, the main road through the township was for packhorses passing between Ulverston and Kendal whilst the others were just tracks for farm carts.

Henry VI gave the Manor of Witherslack to Thomas, Lord Stanley. The first Earl of Derby, and his descendants still hold it. Mrs. Stanley developed Halecat, which was originally built by a retired cotton merchant from Manchester, John B Wanklyn in 1846/47. A Court Leet was held annually at the Derby Arms on the second Tuesday after Trinity to admit new tenants and consider any other grievances or claims relating to the manor and to receive the rents. This continued until 1909 when the Dowager Countess of Derby offered enfranchisement to each of the tenants and the courts were no longer needed.

The present church, school and school house were built in the second half of the 17th century, much information about those times coming from the records of Dean Barwick's Charity. (Dean Barwick was born in Witherslack in 1612, went on the become a Doctor of Divinity at Cambridge. He then became Dean of Durham and later St Paul's, London, where he was buried. The church was built following the terms of his will.) That school house of 1672 cost about £28 and was sufficient for the first incumbent. However, in 1713 it was agreed to build a better one on adjoining land for the then Curate, Rev Richard Ion. It cost £60.

Part of Dean Barwick's bequest included property left in trust for buying a burial ground for the people of Witherslack, which was part of the parish of Beetham. Before then, they had to be carried five miles, crossing over the sands and Kent channel, to the mother church. It was not until 1891 that St Paul's Church became the Parish Church of Witherslack, Meathop and Ulpha and the incumbent became a vicar.

A mill for the customary tenants of the Manor was recorded in 1652. In 1960 it was the last water mill purchased by W & J Pye Ltd of Lancaster. They sold it in 1981 for conversion into homes.

MORECAMBE BAY RAMBLES

From the westbound Witherslack bus stop on the main road, go to the very minor road passing beneath it, seeing the eastbound bus stop to the right, and up to the Derby Arms Hotel at its top. At the crossroads turn right along the road, which used to be the busy main road from Kendal to Barrow.

Follow the road until reaching another crossroads and there turn left. There is some limited parking at the roadside and the round trip walk can be done from here.

Go up the road and on reaching Lower Fell End Farm turn right onto the footpath for Whitbarrow. Follow the roadway through the farmyard and through a field gate from where follow the farm track ahead. It goes up towards the woodland and turns left up the hillside in front of a field gate. Go through a large wooden gate and follow the path in front (25). At the top, it is about forty metres to the left to the permissive path up Whitbarrow.

On reaching the permissive path going up through the woodland, turn right up it, pass a small path coming down from the left, and come to a small bridge. Just after that there is a seat with a good view across to the Bay. Very close by, before reaching the seat, there is a path turning left up the hillside and this is the one to follow, it is waymarked.

BWM21 Whitbarrow Scar.

WALK 21

The path goes to the left as it ascends Whitbarrow. It comes to a wall, which pass through and then turn right for a small wooden gate only a few metres ahead. From the gate, go straight up the earthen woodland track in front.

The woodland is left for more open country, but still with several birches around and then comes out into completely open land. From up here there are views across and down Morecambe Bay. Follow the grassy path ahead; it is a very clear one. The path turns to the left towards the Winster Valley. Witherslack village is seen below and to the left.

Limestone cairns are passed as the path is followed along. The summit is some distance ahead. A wall is seen in front and then the path drops down a little, passing to the right of some limestone rock with its sedimentary deposit lines in it. A Silurian grit erratic stone may be noticed on the left. It is a volcanic rock from another area which was left behind here by a retreating glacier. The wall is crossed at a stone slab stile, so entering the Harvey Nature Reserve.

A cairn is passed on the way to the final two at the summit, one being an ordinary cairn and the other a memorial cairn. About a third of the way along to the summit, just off the path to the right, there is another erratic boulder. It is noticeably different in appearance from the surrounding limestone rock and has different lichens on it.

The Harvey Memorial Cairn, Lord's Seat (28), is reached and there turn left to go down the path, which is a mixture of grass and loose limestone. The path does wind a little but the route is indicated by a number of cairns. It then turns left, looking straight along the side of Whitbarrow and across the Winster Valley. Come to a stile leading to a gap in the wall and the path then drops down quite steeply to the left as it passes down the face of the cliff.

Drop down a normal path as it goes round to the left and through a gap in a wall onto playing fields. There, turn left to go behind the goal to a wooden stile leading onto a grassy farm track, where turn right. The track bears a little to the left to go to some farm buildings seen in front. Just to the left of the buildings is a field gate with a kissing gate by it, leading out to a road.

Follow the road round to the right (26) and up to Witherslack Hall Farm where there is a road for Boland Bridge and Winster. To the left is a very good track which is the bridleway to follow for Halecat. A few metres along the bridleway there is a junction, where follow the main path going to the left.

MORECAMBE BAY RAMBLES

At Lawns House the track splits, the one to use being to the right, away from the houses. The track passes through a field gate. At first it starts through woodland with walls on either side, gradually coming to an open area. There, the track bears off a little to the right, away from the wall. Soon after, it turns further to the right and steadily approaches a wall over to the left. On reaching a field gate, go over a wooden stile by it and straight along the path in front.

On shortly coming to a junction of a farm track to the left and path to the right, follow the path through the trees to the right. Continue dropping down the path, passing a waymarker for a path off to the left.

(From a little cairn, a diversion to Witherslack church can be made by dropping down the path to the left and then turning right to come out onto the road below.)

Continue down the path from the cairn and come out onto a road where turn left. Halecat can be seen over the wall at the far side of the road. Follow the road along and come to the main part of Witherslack village. On coming out at the road by The Forge, turn right. From the crossroads at what was the *Derby Arms Hotel*, follow the minor road down to the bus stops for Kendal (left) and Barrow (right) on the main road.

25. Walk 20 is met at the top of this path.
27. Walk 21 uses the path to here, but in reverse.
28. Walk 20 is met at the cairn.

WALK 21

Bay walks 19, 20 & 21

MORECAMBE BAY RAMBLES

WALK 22, LEVENS BRIDGE, COASTAL WAY, LINDALE OR GRANGE-OVER-SANDS

Easy.
9½ miles, 15¼ km.
Allow 3¾ hours to Lindale.

A mainly coastal walk by reclaimed land.

This walk starts from the bus stops at Levens Bridge. From either, go to the footpath into the woodland on the northern side of the Kent, only a few metres from the entrance to Levens Hall. Follow the path along to a stile by the road. Drop down it onto the permissive path along the edge of the field, at the other side of the hedge from the road. The route comes back onto the road at a wooden stile and there turns left.

On coming to a road junction, turn left and pass down the road, passing Low Levens Farm and in about half a mile come to the buildings of High Sampool on the left. Just beyond, there is a junction where the tarred road continues ahead, but turn onto the untarred road to the right. It comes out onto the main road where turn left to cross the River Gilpin and then left again at the next junction. The road is a straight reclamation road.

At High Foulshaw the road goes right for a few metres and then left again. It is followed for another two hundred metres until, just after passing under a pylon line, turn left at a field gate and go straight across the field by the hedge on the left towards the embankment to be seen in front.

Go through a field gate at the end and turn right along the track just below the embankment. Pass through a field gate and then go straight ahead where the embankment veers off to the left. At the end of the track go through a wooden kissing gate leading up onto the embankment and turn right along its top. Seen across the Kent Estuary are Milnthorpe and Sandside.

The embankment is followed for two miles until a natural rocky point, Birkswood Point, is reached, where pass through the field gate spanning the embankment. A track is followed into a field and the farm track is followed over the point.

Continue along the track over a further short stretch of embankment and then go through a metal field gate and pass Crag Cottage. Just after passing the cottage the path goes upwards and there, just before reaching a large ash tree, a sign shows that the route to follow is over to the right towards a small wooden ladder stile. Go over the stile, and then cross a bridge spanning the

WALK 22

main drain from Foulshaw Moss. Another stile is then crossed, where bear left towards a stream, but only for a few metres before turning to the right to go towards the end of the embankment in front, where there is a hedge to its left, a fence to its right and a stile onto it.

As the embankment ends, carry straight on ahead and then along a bit more embankment at the end of which is a wooden ladder stile into the next field. Cross straight over the field to a wooden ladder stile by a field gate, it leading out onto a road where turn left.

Jeffreys' map of Westmorland of 1770 shows a road from Wilson House, through 'Medup' (Meathop) and 'Ulvay' (Ulpha) to Witherslack. Otherwise, the whole of the coastal plain between the Kent and the Winster is shown as mosses. The name is thought to derive from Old English referring to the middle of the valley or marshland. At the time of the map, it was certainly in the middle of a vast area of moss land. The moss became a nature reserve in 1939. In 2001, along with Foulshaw Moss and Nichols Moss, it became part of Witherslack Mosses and is an SSSI.

Meathop Grange, which is now housing, was formerly an isolation hospital, very appropriate for somewhere so cut off from the main stream of life. It was to here that many patients suffering from tuberculosis were sent to recover.

The very minor road is followed to a junction where turn right for Meathop. There, at a junction, the main road drops down to the right and the one to follow is the minor road straight ahead into a wood. Pass the entrance to Meathop Grange and then come to Low Meathop on the right.

Go down the roadway, straight through the farmyard, and then continue along the good track in front. The track suddenly changes from being an unsurfaced roadway into a broad grassy one and shortly turns left towards Lindale. The track ends. Go to a wooden gate that drops the path down to a wooden bridge spanning the River Winster. Cross the bridge to another wooden gate onto the path. Pass through another gate and turn right along the broad, grassy path in front, it formerly having been a continuous road across the river.

Come out at a wooden field gate and onto a road where turn left for Lindale. On reaching the village, turn left onto the Grange-over-Sands road and a few metres ahead are the bus shelters for the local and Barrow to Kendal services, close by the Wilkinson monument. By continuing straight ahead along the road, Grange-over-Sands station is about a mile and three quarters distant.

MORECAMBE BAY RAMBLES

The winding River Winster between Meathop and Lindale was the old boundary between Westmorland and Lancashire. The river passes close to Castlehead, which was formerly known as 'Atterpile Castle'. It was apparently a stronghold for the Romans, seventy-five of their coins having been found here, and later of the Saxons and the Vikings. It would have been a good stronghold before the reclamation of some of the mosses and the building of the railway embankments resulted in the tides no longer coming up to it.

For a while, John Wilkinson, the ironmaster, was buried at Castlehead, which he had bought around 1765 and where he had his house built. A subsequent purchaser of the house had Wilkinson's iron coffin removed and reburied in the churchyard. That was perhaps a more appropriate place to bury him as the remains of a bloomery were found close to the old wall of St Paul's church during an extension in 1912. An iron monument to Wilkinson stands by the road to Grange.

Before the by-pass road was built, Lindale Hill was a notorious blackspot for fatal accidents. In winter it became almost impassable when there was snow and ice about. Heavy articulated lorries jacknifed when trying to round the corner by the Royal Oak. Now, the village is quiet once more, as it must have been before the advent of motor traffic.

BWM22 Wilkinson Monument, Lindale.

BWC09 Harvey Memorial Cairn and rainbow, Whitbarrow.
BWC10 Cartmel Priory.

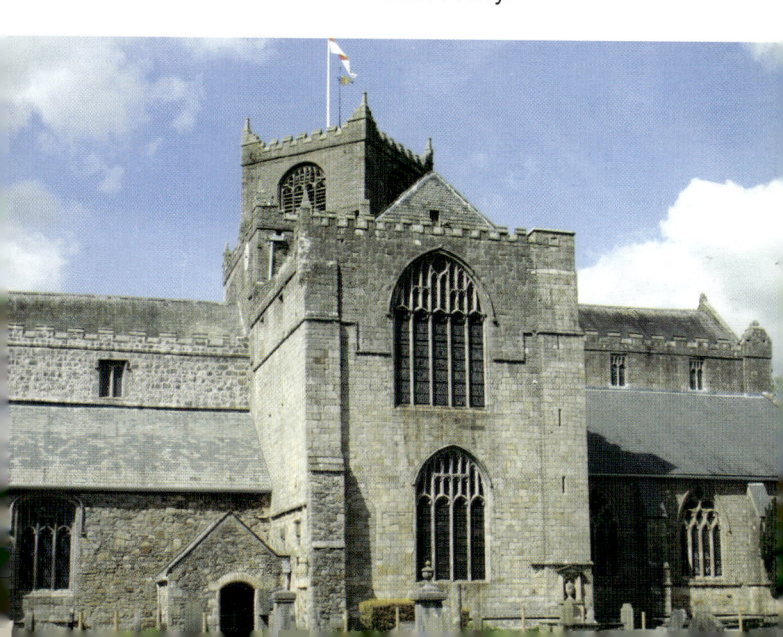

BWC11 Cark.
BWC12 Former sea lock and Ulverston Canal.

BWC13 Down to Bardsea beach.
BWC14 Great Urswick.

BWC15 Leece pond.
BWC16 Biggar Bank.

WALK 22

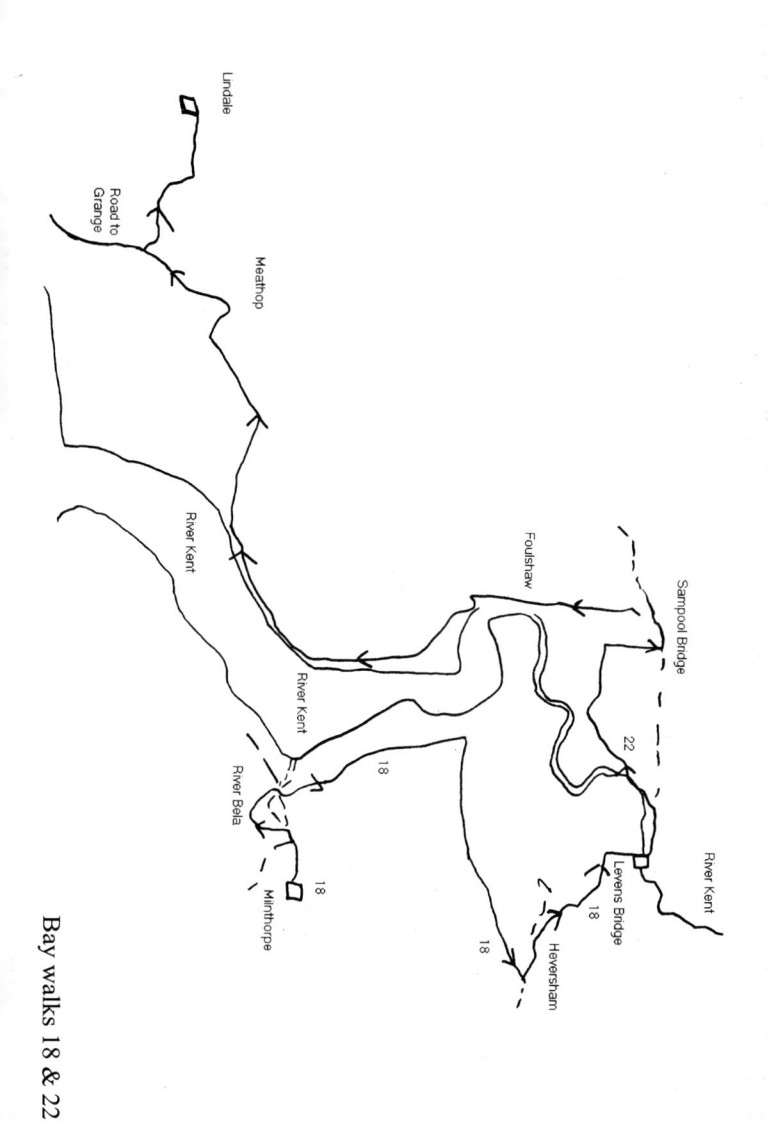

Bay walks 18 & 22

MORECAMBE BAY RAMBLES

WALK 23, GRANGE, HAMPSFELL HOSPICE, LINDALE, GRANGE

Generally easy but can be slippery on wet limestone.
6 miles, 9½ km.
Allow 3½ hours.

Climb a limestone hillside to a viewpoint before going into woodland.

It was the coming of the railway in 1857 that led to the main development of Grange-over-Sands. Mannex Directory of 1851 has no separate entry for the village, but it is included with Broughton township, of which it was a part although detached. The directory shows very few businesses in Grange, unlike fifteen years later. By that time, it had become a parish in its own right, the first incumbent being the Rev Wilson Rigg, who arrived by coach across the Bay and very nearly drowned when the coach sank.

Grange was a granary for Cartmel Priory and a stone believed to be part of the original building can be seen in the sunken War Memorial gardens by the ornamental gardens with the lake. Nearby, believed to be roughly below where the "Commodore" now stands, was the port, but it was only a small affair.

The ornamental gardens are on the site of an old creek washed by the tides from which it became cut off following the building of the railway embankment. The gardens were nearly lost to development in 1892 and were only saved by the chairman of the town council using his casting vote. The principle source of water before the coming of piped water in 1879 was Picklefoot Spring, which still keeps on flowing. Before the gardens were constructed, the tides covered it twice a day, but shortly after they retreated it was pure again as though there had been no salt water near it. The people of the town then went with buckets to draw sufficient supplies until after the next high water.

The oldest building in Grange is Hard Crag Hall, dating from 1563, and which was once the home of John Wilkinson, the ironmaster. Later, Beatrix Potter regularly visited the Hall, which had its own piggery and it was on one of those occasions that she met the original of Pigling Bland. It is believed that the present library occupies the site of the piggery.

The railway line was originally single track, but was doubled in 1863 following the acquisition of the Ulverstone & Lancaster Railway by the Furness Railway. Until then, the station was a small affair but it was replaced by the present station, which was designed by Mr E G Paley, architect, of Lancaster. His design is in keeping with the close by Grange Hotel, also designed by him. The high tides washed the embankment on which the railway was built, including the seaward side of the station. The promenade was not built until 1904.

Now, there is an extensive saltmarsh at Grange, but this only started to appear from the 1970's. Where sheep now graze, boats once sailed, bringing trippers to Clare House Pier, which stood quite close to the café and the former swimming baths.

From Grange-over–Sands station, turn left to go into the ornamental gardens and then follow a path round the lake either to the left or to the right until the shelter on the far side is reached. There, turn up past the toilets to the road. Cross the road and just to the left are two stone pillars on either side of a driveway by a cottage. Go through them and either up the steps or the driveway to the retirement home in front. On reaching it, pass up the path to the left of the building to reach another path and a shelter up some steps above it. Climb the steps past the shelter and turn right onto the path behind and follow this path round at the edge of woodland, ignoring two others dropping down to the right

Pass through a large metal gate and then along the path by the fence on the right. As the fence drops below, continue on the main path, which then swings right round to the left, ignoring one going straight ahead. Another track is shortly joined (it is on another way from the shelter) and turn right to reach a large metal field gate onto Hampsfell Road, where turn right.

Follow the road round as it turns to the left and goes up hill. At its end there is a wooden field gate to pass through and then bear right across the track to a wooden kissing gate. From it, follow the grassy path upwards, bearing to the right. There are good views of Morecambe Bay looking back. Ahead there is a wall with a stone step stile to cross, then go straight up the hillside in front to reach another wall where a wooden ladder stile is seen. Cross it and turn left to follow the path over limestone pavement. It then becomes grassy as it makes its way up the Fell, bearing a little over to the right.

From the top of Hampsfell there is a view over the whole of the old parish of Cartmel and to the Lake District Fells in one direction and over Morecambe Bay and beyond in the other direction. The Rev Thomas Remington, who was vicar at Cartmel Priory for 30 odd years from 1830, had a limestone tower, known as Hampsfell Hospice, built as a refuge for the benefit of visitors and other people in 1834. He so loved the fell that he climbed it every day.

MORECAMBE BAY RAMBLES

On top of the Hospice is an indicator showing the various lndmarks to be seen on a clear day.

BWM23 Morecambe Bay from Lindale.

On reaching Hampsfell Hospice, with its excellent views all around the Bay and to the Lake District, turn right along a grassy path with the top of the limestone rocks on the right. Just beyond the top of the fell the path, which is actually a bridleway from here, bears a little to the right. On reaching a dip down towards more limestone in front, turn right at the bottom of the dip to go between the two outcrops of limestone. Pass a waymarker and in front, see a stone wall crossing the path. Go through a gate in the wall and then follow the path along amongst the bracken.

Follow the bridleway round. It turns towards the left as it drops down towards the woodland below and then turns right again, this is as it drops down to the track which can be seen running along by the wall bounding the woodland. Once under the pylon line the path goes left again as it drops down to the wall, where there is a gap which is ignored (29). Turn left to go along by the wall. On coming to a wall descending the fell, cross it at the wooden ladder stile by a field gate and then continue straight along the track as before.

WALK 23

Further on, a stile takes the path through the wall and to a junction of paths where take the one to the right. Follow it through the woodland to where there is a field over to the left and a stone stile leading into it. Go through that stile and along by the wall on the right. (If that turning is overshot, you end up in a garden.) Come to a field gate, pass through it, and then continue down the path to a road where turn right.

At the end of the road, enter the field in front and cross over the grassy path bearing to the left. On reaching the left-hand corner of the field there is a wooden kissing gate to pass through. Continue following the grassy path down the next field, through another kissing gate and then along a woody stretch to some stone steps.

Go up the steps and a few metres ahead there is the end of a private road. Cross straight over it to go through a large metal kissing gate, with Lindale to be seen down below. Drop down the field and follow the path to Lindale, dropping down some steps and going through a squeeze stile on the way. Pass just to the left of the first dwelling and out onto a cul de sac and drop down it to the proper road at Lingarth, which is on a route for Kendal and Barrow direction buses.

For Lindale village, turn left along the road for a few metres and then take the first road dropping down to the right. Pass straight down it to come out at the main road through the village. There, turn right for the Post Office and stores and the road for Grange-over-Sands and Levens Bridge. On reaching the roundabout there, turn right for the main bus stops.

For a walk back to Grange-over-Sands, turn right along the footpath close to the right-hand bus shelter. Go up it, over the open field area and in the far right corner there is a gateway leading out onto a road. Turn left, pass Meadowcroft and then go up some stone steps to a scrubby slope. Follow the path by the scrubland on the right and shortly come to another path. Here, turn right along it and come out at a squeeze stile at the back of the school. Pass by the playground to another squeeze stile and then out onto the road used earlier, where turn left to follow the outward route.

At the top of the hill, turn left for a few metres and then right past the houses at Lyngarth again. Pass the last of the houses and onto the path and then to some stone steps on the right, leading to a stone squeeze stile. Go straight up the field by the wall on the left. Pass through a large metal kissing gate, across the roadway, and continue along the path. It drops down some stone steps to a wooden kissing gate at the bottom. From there, follow the grassy field path that bears a little to the right and, once over it, bear quite well over to the right towards the houses, etc. See a metal field gate with a stone

MORECAMBE BAY RAMBLES

squeeze stile to its left leading out onto the roadway. Follow the roadway for a short distance to pass Stonegarth and straight after there turn left onto the path. Follow the path along, through a wooden field gate and into a field. Pass along by the wall on the left to a stone squeeze stile where turn right.

Shortly, a junction is reached and there take the left-hand path. Cross a wall and follow the path along into Eggerslack Wood. On reaching a junction, go to the left, the path to the right leads to the outward path.

At the next junction, only a few metres ahead, turn right and follow the path to the next junction where take the main path to the left. Pass a minor path to the left, staying on the main one. At the next junction, ignore the first path to the left but continue for another few metres to where a main path comes in from the right. Turn left along it and come to another junction, where turn left. Follow the main path, ignoring others to the left and right, and then turn left to drop down to a roadway (30).

Across the roadway are some stone steps to go down and continue along the path, crossing another roadway on the way, down some more stone steps and continue to a stone squeeze stile out onto a road, where turn right. (Note, this last section of the way through the woodland is over limestone which can be very slippery when wet.) Follow the road through to Grange-over-Sands and at a junction see the station and bus stops to the left.

29. Walk 24 comes across here.
30. Walk 24 ascends this path.

WALK 24, GRANGE-OVER-SANDS, CARTMEL, GRANGE-OVER-SANDS

Moderate.
6 miles, 9½ km.
Allow 3¾ hours.

Cross a limestone hill to the attractive old village of Cartmel.

From Grange station, go along the footway by the railings of the Ornamental Gardens up to the junction with the road for Ulverston, which is apparently in either direction. Cross that road and turn right. After passing the last of the houses on the left, only about five minutes away, turn left at a squeeze stile onto the footpath through the woodland (30), the first part of which can be slippery when wet. Go straight up the path, crossing two roadways on the way. On having crossed the second roadway, take the path going to the left, it being marked for Hampsfell.

BWM24 Ornamental gardens, Grange-over-Sands.

MORECAMBE BAY RAMBLES

The path quickly swings to the right and then turns left again. Continue along the main path, there are others to the left and right. In due course, it comes to some stone steps leading over a wall and out onto Hampsfell (29). Go straight up the track in front for a few metres and, as it turns right, go straight ahead, there is a waymarker. It is a good limestone area. Follow the grassy path up the hillside, going to the left of the limestone in front.

Continue over the grassy path to further limestone rocks in front and to a wall where there is a stone slab stile to cross. From it, continue upwards with the wall on the right. On reaching the top of the wall, bear left for Hampsfell Hospice a short way ahead, crossing over limestone pavement to reach it.

Go straight past the Hospice (31) and onto some limestone land. Go a short way to the right and then turn to the left to drop down the grassy fell slope. On the way down, there is a very good view to Cartmel over to the left and the Bay beyond. As the Fell is descended, see ahead Longlands with trees round it and a square enclosure in front. You have to go to the left of there to Borwick's Aynsome beyond and by a road, but the first part of the descent is towards Longlands.

The path then goes to the left and before turning right to drop down the hillside straight opposite Longlands before coming to another grassy track quite close to a wall, where turn left. Go through a gateway to the right (there is a waymarker) and follow the grassy path on the left. This is only for a few metres before it turns right to drop right down the field. (Strictly, the right of way goes round the field following the walls on your left.) A gateway by a field gate in the fence at the bottom leads into the next field and there go straight down it and then by the wall on the left to Borwick's Aynsome farmyard.

Go through the farmyard, passing through two field gates, and out onto the road, where turn left towards Cartmel. On reaching Cartmel, if wishing to see the village, take the first turning right, but the walk itself continues straight ahead (32). On reaching a triangular green, turn left onto the road for Grange-over-Sands, Haggs Road.

Pass the last of the houses and a few metres beyond there is a stile through the wall on the left, leading into a field. Follow the grassy path up the field, taking a line that is roughly a continuation of the road which had been followed to here, and with a good view back to Cartmel on the way. At the top of the path there is a wooden ladder stile leading onto a golf course. Follow the marked path and beware of golf balls. The path bears upwards to the right and is clear to follow to a wooden ladder stile leading off the golf course and back onto the Fell.

WALK 24

Follow the grassy path along, with the golf course just over to the right. Where the path splits, take the lower one by the fence. Cross a stone step stile onto a roadway, cross it, and go over another stone step stile and across the corner of the field in front. There, come to some stone steps leading up onto the road (the same one used out of Cartmel) and turn left for Grange-over-Sands.

The road drops down quite steeply into Grange, passing Hard Crag Hall on the way. At the bottom, come to the library and then cross the road ahead. Turn left after the churchto go down the main street, past several of the shops, and either continue round the road to the station or go through the ornamental gardens.

29. Walk 23 passes along the wall to the right.
30. Walk 23 descends this path.
31. Walks 23 and 25 come to the Hospice.
32. Walk 25 goes into Cartmel village.

MORECAMBE BAY RAMBLES

WALK 25, GRANGE-OVER-SANDS, HAMPSFELL, CARTMEL, CARK

Generally easy, but can need a little extra care in places at times.
5¼ miles, 8½ km. Plus another kilometre return for the diversion to Hampsfell Hospice.
Allow 3½ hours.

Cross over a limestone hill to the attractive village of Cartmel and then along a broad valley to the former mill village of Cark.

From Grange-over-Sands station, turn left into the ornamental gardens and then go round the lake to the shelter on the far side, the route followed to there does not matter. Go up onto the road, cross it, and go along the driveway between two stone pillars to the left of the cottage by them. Either follow the driveway round or go up the steps to the retirement home in front and then pass along its left-hand side to a path above. From it, go up to the shelter looking out over Morecambe Bay, pass to the left of it and turn left along the path at the top.

In a few metres there is a path to the right to be followed; it comes to a metal gate leading out onto Hampsfell Road, where turn left. A few metres along the road there are the remains of an old limekiln and just past there a tarred track goes up to the right, it being for Charney Well and Yewbarrow Wood. At a junction, ignore the path to the left, but go above the remains of the limekiln. After this, the tarred road swings to the left, but the path goes straight on ahead into the woodland.

In a few metres there is a small wooden gate to pass through and by it a junction of paths, where take the one on the right to pass along the edge of the woodland. Follow it along, through a more open area and then onto a main track going to the left. It comes out onto a roadway, which is followed for a short distance to another roadway going to the right. Turn onto it and come out onto another road and there turn left down it for a few metres to where a sign indicates that a footpath to the right is for Hampsfell. Turn up it, passing by a garden on the left and other land on the right.

The well-used path is then followed along towards the farm at Spring Bank. On reaching there, turn right along the wall and come to a stone slab stile. Cross it and then go up the farm track in front towards some houses above. There, turn right along the road and shortly come to a junction where turn left. On coming to a gateway on the right, opposite the end of the houses, go through it and onto the Fell.

WALK 25

Follow the grassy path up the fell in front, it disappearing to become just open fell. Continue upwards towards a wall in front and on reaching it go through a gateway. Of the two very clear grassy paths going over to the right, take the left-hand one. Follow it ahead, with some good views, and then it dips down before going up again. Here, there is a path dropping down to the left, which is ignored if going to Hampsfell Hospice (31), but turn down it if going straight to Cartmel.

Continue on up the good, clear grassy path for another few minutes, pass through a slab stile in a wall, coming out at the Hospice with its views all around. Turn back to follow the outward path, through some limestone clints and grikes and onto the grassy path. At a junction, ignore the path to the left, but keep on going down to where the one being used rises and there, at the indicator, turn right for Cartmel, which is then seen ahead and below.

On shortly coming to a junction, take the path to the left. Go through a metal kissing gate into a field and then down it by the wall on the right. When well into the field, bear a little to the left towards a metal field gate that is to be seen in the fence in front. Pass through it into the following field where bear left to go over towards the right-hand end of Pit Farm seen in front. There is a metal kissing gate to the right of a field gate to go through and then turn left along the track for a few metres. Turn left to go through a gateway into another field, the remains of the stile no longer being used, and towards the hedge on the left.

Pass straight down that field by the hedge until near the end when go a little to the right to pass through a wooden gate and through what is virtually a tunnel caused by a wall on one side and hedge on the other. This comes out onto the road (32), where turn left to the next junction and there turn right.

Cartmel comes from Old Norse meaning a sandbank by rocky ground, the rocky ground being Hampsfell. Passing through it is the small River Eea, a name that perhaps arose from its small size as it comes from the Old English for 'river'.

The village is famous for its beautiful priory church, which was founded by William Marshall, Earl of Pembroke, between 1190 and 1196, and is dedicated to St Mary and St Michael. Unfortunately, the early records of the church and its possessions have all been lost. The priory had never to become an abbey and had to have a priest for the people of Cartmel. This latter condition saved the church at the Dissolution of the Monasteries, when the order was given that it "stand still".

MORECAMBE BAY RAMBLES

The stonework in the chancel is very elaborate and was carved over several years at a time when money was no object; William Marshall was a very rich man.

An unusual feature of the priory is the Bell Tower which is in two sections, the upper section lying at an angle of 45 degrees to the lower section. This construction showed great engineering skill as it stopped the lower arches from bursting upwards. The massive pillars at the Crossing in the centre of the building support the tower,

The choir stalls date back to 1430-40 with the screens and canopies being from the early 1600's. Only one of the misericords has been lost. They are all different, each having a main central carving with smaller ones flanking them. Included are real and imaginary beasts, foliage and even a mermaid.

The Harrington Tomb is actually the remains of a chantry chapel in memory of Lord John Harrington and Joan, his wife, and includes their effigies.

The Gatehouse would not be the original entrance to Cartmel and its church, but dates from the 14th century. It has housed the school and for many years housed the local court; the courtroom measuring only 17ft by 17ft 5 ins. Following restoration in 1922, the building was gifted to the National Trust.

Close to the Gatehouse is the Village Shop, well known for sticky toffee pudding, and beyond is the racecourse.

BWM25 Cartmel Square and Gatehouse.

WALK 25

On reaching the Priory Church, follow the footpath to the left, passing the main church entrance and come out onto a road. Turn right and pass through the centre of Cartmel, passing to the left of the Village Shop, which is famous for its sticky toffee pudding, and come out onto the racecourse roadway. Go through the car park and then straight ahead along the main path in front, its crossing over the racetrack.

Keep straight on along this very good track, through woodland at Lane Park, to High Bank Side where, at a junction, take the track to the left. Follow the tarred roadway along, past Low Bank Side and see the main road below and the houses of Cark in front. The road is joined at a metal field gate, where turn right.

Pass two roads going off to the left and then come to a junction where take the road to the left, dropping down into Cark village. At the bottom of the road, turn left, pass the Engine Inn, and in about a quarter of a mile come to the railway station and bus stops.

The 'Engine Inn' is not named after the railway but an engine in the nearby Big Mill and was formerly called the Fire Engine Inn.

Until 1782 Cark was said to be one of the 'prettiest little rural villages in the north of England.' Until then, Cark Beck, as the River Eea is called here, was crossed by just one bridge near the inn. There was also a wooden bridge and stepping stones across its waters. The course of the river was changed with the building of the mill, an artificial channel being made for it.

To prevent smoke from the "fire engine", as the steam engine was known, blackening the mill, there was an underground archway constructed to High Row and then it ascended a large, square chimney. The noise of the engine could be heard for miles. Originally the mill was used for the manufacture of cotton goods, but got into financial difficulties and closed around 1808. Later, in 1816, it became a corn mill.

Above the western bank of the river were three rows of cottages for mill workers, Low Row, Middle Row and High Row. Middle Row has now been demolished, but the other two rows remain, but have been modernised. The mill had changed Cark from being a small rural village into an industrial village.

31. Walks 24 and 25 visit the Hospice.
32. Walk 24 returns direct to Grange.

MORECAMBE BAY RAMBLES

WALK 26, GRANGE-OVER-SANDS, KENTS BANK, CARK

Easy.
6 miles, 9¾ km.
Allow 3 hours.

A very pleasant walk that is mainly coastal.

Kents Bank is one end of the Cross Bay route that was regularly used by coaches until the coming of the railway. Guide's Farm, the home of the Guide across the treacherous sands of Morecambe Bay is passed on the walk to here. The Abbot of Furness Abbey used to stay at the original Abbot Hall, built around 1160, on his way across the sands from Ulverston to the Abbey's Yorkshire estates.

Now, walkers use the cross sands route in the summer months, the Guide being Cedric Robinson. The walks generally start from Arnside and set off across the Bay from White Creek. Walkers generally catch a return train from the unmanned Kents Bank Station, a far cry from when it had a Station Master and staff.

The present Abbot Hall, dating from 1840, is a Methodist guest house.

BWM26 The promenade, Grange-over-Sands.

WALK 26

On leaving Grange-over-Sands station, go under the railway lines and onto the promenade where turn right to follow it all the way to its end. There, pass under the railway line. Continue along the path to the road ahead and turn up it to the first turning left, Cart Lane, and go along it. At the end of the lane, follow the footpath ahead, it being between the railway and a field.

The path ends by going up some steps to a road, where turn left down to Kents Bank station and there turn right to go straight up the hilly road. On reaching the main road, take the very minor road to the left, Jack Hill, and drop down it to the lower part of Allithwaite. At the bottom of the road, turn left to pass along the farm and then through the farmyard, through the gateways and along the track towards Humphrey Head, which is the promontory to be seen in front.

Allithwaite comes from 'Eilifir' a Norse settler and probably a farmer and his 'thwaite' was probably a clearing in the woodland around. The soil around the village is fertile.

The church, dedicated to St Mary, was built in 1865 from monies provided by Miss Mary Winifred Lambert, who was extremely rich. The village had not been able to afford a church earlier.

According to a local tradition, the last wolf in England was killed near Allithwaite. There is a seventy-five verse Victorian poem about the killing, but it is very fanciful.

Humphrey Head is a carboniferous limestone headland noted for its plants. Now, a trickle of water is all that remains of its once famous spa. Waters were taken from here to be sold in Morecambe.

Towards the end of the field that has been entered, see the stile to cross between two field gates. Go straight along the next field by the hedge on the left; cross a wooden stile into the following field and again go straight along it. At the top left corner of the field, by a tree, there is a footbridge to cross before the following field is crossed alongside the ditch on its left.

At the end of the field a staggered stone squeeze stile leads onto a roadway with a wooden stile into the field on the opposite side. Follow the path by the fence on the left. Bear right at the end of the field to go under the railway line and into another field. It is crossed to a gate at the end, through it and immediately to the left there is a stone stile with some steps leading down to the beach.

MORECAMBE BAY RAMBLES

Turn right along the beach, with Humphrey Head just in front. Go along by the wall on the right and at its end there is a small gate by a field gate to pass through. Follow the track along and come out onto a road. If not going to Humphrey Head, turn right along the road. However, most walkers will, time permitting, want to visit Humphrey Head, in which case turn left.

The entrance to Humphrey Head, which is private land but with permissive paths, is just by the path that has been followed to here. Go up the driveway, but before reaching the fence and entrance to the Outdoor Centre turn right straight up the slope, passing through a fence on the way. There are views of reclamation land below. The southern slope of the headland is steeper as it drops down towards the rocks below, and these can be crossed to Humphrey Head Point. On the way back, bear over to the right and in the wall in front is a ladder stile leading into the woodland. Follow the path through the woodland and come out into the open close to the Outdoor Centre. Go along by the fence to come out at the entrance.

Wraysholme Tower is a pele tower that may have been built as protection for Cartmel Priory. However, if that was so, it did not remain under the control of the monks for long as just over a century later it was in the possession of the Harrington family of Aldingham and it is generally believed they built it around 1485. Later, the tower passed into the hands of Sir Edward Stanley of Flodden Field fame. Now, it is just an outbuilding to Wraysholme Farm.

Returning to the road, continue straight along it. See Wraysholme Tower to the right. At the road junction not far ahead, take the road to the left. This is followed to its end, where turn right (33). Go straight up the road into Flookburgh. There, cross over the square and Market Street (there are bus stops to the right) and go straight up Station Road, passing Flookburgh Parish Church on the way to Cark and Cartmel station, where there are further bus stops.

33. Walk 27 goes down the road to the left.

WALK 26

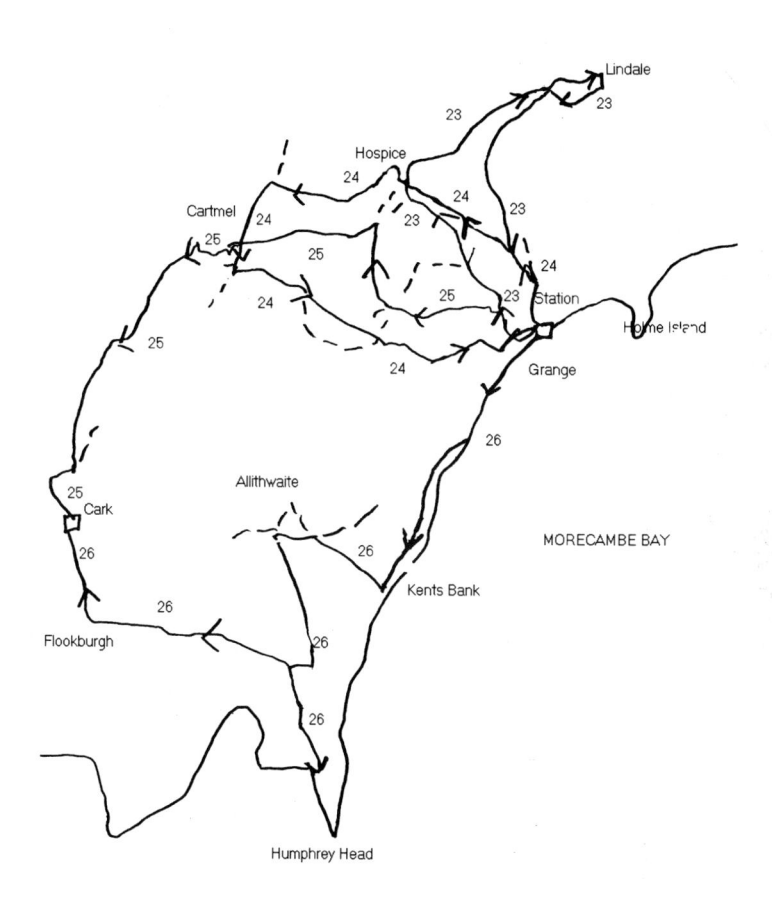

Bay walks 23, 24, 25 & 26

MORECAMBE BAY RAMBLES

WALK 27, CARK, FLOOKBURGH, THE COAST, CARK

Conditions along this route vary according to the weather and tidal deposits, but it is basically easy. It is a largely coastal walk from the fishing village of Flookburgh to the former mill village of Cark.
5¼ miles, 8½ km.
Allow 2½ hours.

Flookburgh is still a village from which fishermen set out onto Morecambe Bay. It was also a market town, its first market charter being granted by Edward I in 1278, enabling markets to be held each Tuesday. The market has long since lapsed.

BWM27 FISHING TRAILERS, SANDGATE, FLOOKBURGH.

In "Annals of Cartmel", R J Stockdale tells of a major fire around 1686, which destroyed a great part of the town. It was apparently caused by 'the negligence of a woman who had left hempe or some other combustible matter too neare the fire wch. Bursting out in the thatch and increased by the violence of a mightie hott and drie wind' burned down twenty-two dwelling houses and many other buildings. It also destroyed the orchards.

The village has a large square because the churchyard that was here was removed about 1920. The church, which was apparently an ugly building, was replaced by the present church in 1900 and was subsequently demolished. St John's Church was designed by Paley and Austin of Lancaster.

Before the coming of the railways, the main route from Lancaster to Ulverston ran through Flookburgh. Traffic landed at Sandgate and then followed what is now a minor road to Flookburgh. In 1768/9 over £87 was spent on widening the road, heavy expenditure for the time. More was spent in the early 1800's. From about 1810, by when the roads and bridges at Cark had been much improved, coaches ceased to use the route and went via Cark instead.

In 1797 an area of West Plain was enclosed, reclaiming the land, which was sometimes flooded up to Flookburgh, by the tides. In 1808 a further embankment was completed, claiming over 600 acres of marsh and buildings were constructed on that land. In 1828 the River Leven changed its course, cut into the foundations of the embankments, which collapsed and returned the land to marsh. Now only a few metres of the West Plain embankment remain.

Canon Winder is so called because it was once owned by the canons of Cartmel priory. Its main entrance, with stone piers topped by stone balls, fronts onto the sands; the 1845 OS map shows no landward route to the hall.

Most of the Lake District can be seen in the space of an hour or so at Flookburgh. There, the Lakeland Miniature Village has models of many well known and some not so well known buildings.

From Cark station, turn left along the road, passing Flookburgh Parish Church. Come out onto Market Street, which is crossed, and then go over to the far left-hand corner of the square. Go straight down the road (33) and in about a mile come to where it swings to the left at West Plain Farm. There, pass across the cattle grid in front and onto the foreshore, where turn right. The path is straight along the top of the reclamation embankment of 1797. Pass a short spur to the left that is all that remains of the 1808 embankment and soon afterwards drop down onto the shore itself.

Follow the head of the shore, a marshland area with a wall on the right; cross a stile through a fence and continue along the path. Ulverston is seen over to the left. Cross another stile and keep on along the shore until reaching a track used by fishing tractors where turn onto it. Pass Canon Winder with its large gateway leading out onto the beach.

MORECAMBE BAY RAMBLES

The path is followed, over Strand Bridge spanning the main drain bringing the waters from West Plain at the next farm, Sand Gate, coming to a roadway turning up to the right. Follow it, past the farm and then, as the road starts to bear right, there is a track to the left. Follow that track for about half a mile to Cark, it crossing a bridge over the railway line on the way.

The track comes out at The Fold where turn right to drop down to the main road through the village, where there are bus stops by the Engine Inn. Turn right along the main road, cross the railway line, and come to the station.

33. Walk 26 comes up here from a junction on the left.

WALK 28

WALK 28, CARK, HAVERTHWAITE

Moderate.
6½ miles, 10¼ km.
Allow 4 hours.

Leave the coast behind to enter the southern fringe of the Lake District.

Holker Hall was largely rebuilt in the 1720s and it was then that the formal garden was laid out. The West Wing is another Paley and Austin design, it having been rebuilt following a disastrous fire in 1871. The building is one of their finest works.

The original Holker Hall was built in the 1500s by the Preston family. It passed on through the Lowthers to the Cavendish family, who own it to this day. It has never been sold, but passed by inheritance through the female line. The Hall and grounds are open to the public roughly April to October except Saturday and in early June it hosts the Holker Garden Festival.

On leaving Cark and Cartmel station, turn right to pass through Cark village and follow the road to Holker Hall. Pass the entrance to the Hall and come to a crossroads by a water trough. There, turn up the road to the right and in about a third of a mile come to a gate by a cattle grid. Go through the field gate in front and then along by the wall on the left, at the other side of which is woodland. Follow the good track along until it reaches some woodland in front. Looking back, there is a good view of the Bay.

On reaching the woodland, turn to follow the track as it goes to the left and at its end go through a field gate and then follow the grassy path straight ahead. The path rises towards a pylon, just before which there is another farm track, where turn right. On reaching a gate do not go through it but turn left to follow the wall, which is then on the right. Go through a gateway in a fence, there is a waymarker, and continue following the track for another few metres to where another waymarker shows the route which bears off to the right to continue fairly close to the wall.

From here, the walk is turning inland, away from the Levens Estuary. Pass a path going up the hillside and then come to a gate to go through; there is a Coastal Way signpost. Follow the grassy path along as it goes leftwards. The track starts to bear left towards some farm buildings. At this point it is left to bear to the right towards a field gate and then down a roadway by some caravans. Come out onto another roadway and go straight ahead along it to its end at Burns Farm and enter the farmyard.

On the right, see a field gate and go over to it; there is a Coastal Way sign. The track drops down from the gate and is followed for just over a hundred metres to a junction where take the left-hand path to Speel Bank. Follow the grassy track along, pass through a field gate and go straight ahead to another field gate and then cross the field ahead to yet another metal field gate. Continue along the grassy path by the wall on the right, which is soon topped by a hawthorn hedge.

Part way along, go through a gateway into the next field, there is a waymarker, and continue to follow the same wall along, but with it now on the left. Pass through another metal field gate in the wall reached in front and then straight across the field. Follow the path along by a wall, which has been joined on the right and then there is another metal field gate to go through. Turn right through another field gate in front (there are a number around here, but there are signs) and onto a farm track.

The farmyard at Speel Bank is then passed through and out onto a roadway, which is followed for only a few metres before turning left to go up to and over a ladder stile. From it, follow a wall on the left for a few metres and then continue following the grassy path ahead; the path then bears leftwards up towards the woodland. A wall comes into view in front, it having a large wooden field gate to pass through.

The path is then followed amongst some bracken and with a wall on the left and trees on the right. Keep following it along as it goes through some woodland and then comes out onto open, rocky country with a glimpse of the Leven Estuary to the left. A grassy track is joined and followed, one going off to the right being ignored. Another grassy track coming up from below is joined and a waymarker shows that you turn to the right to go straight up that main track and come to another Coastal Way signpost.

Keep on following the main track, there are others around. Bear over towards a wall on the left, watching out for a stone step stile over it, the stile having a wooden handrail by it.

On having crossed the stile, the path is diagonally over to the left for a few metres to where a metal field gate is seen. Once through that gate, turn left (do not follow the main path straight ahead) and follow the grassy path. Shortly, Grassgarth is seen in front. Drop down the grassy path as it goes towards the pylon line and see a field gate below, near to Grassgarth. As the path is descended towards the gate, it first drops down to the right and then turns round to the left.

Go through the field gate at the bottom and out onto a road that is crossed to a wooden kissing gate a little to the right. From the gate, the path drops down to the right to cross a stream by a wooden plank bridge and then up the field on the far side of it, straight behind Grassgarth. The path then turns left to go just below the wall in front and at the end pass through the metal field gate in a wall and then go straight up the path in front. There is a very good view of the Leven Estuary just before entering woodland. Follow the clear path through the woodland and then come out into the open again after passing through a metal gate. Turn left and follow the grassy path round the hillside, again with a good view of the Leven Estuary.

Follow the path round as it turns to the right and shortly Bigland Tarn comes into view. Follow the path with the Tarn below to the right and come to a gateway from which drop down to near by the Tarn. Ahead, before reaching a field gate in a fence, turn left. Follow the grassy path, there is a waymarker, and drop steadily downwards. Two other paths going off to the left are passed on the way down before entering the woodland further down, with a stream below on the right. Go through a wooden gate and continue dropping down the path which becomes more grassy than stony as it passes through bracken. An open vista across to Backbarrow is passed.

BWM28 Bigland Tarn, near Haverthwaite.

Cross over a quite broad track and then down the path in front, which can also be occupied by a stream. It comes out onto a road where turn right to pass a minor junction (34) and then cross the bridge over the river to a

MORECAMBE BAY RAMBLES

footpath going by it to the right (35). Follow that path to the kissing gate at the end and then turn left up to the road, where turn right through Haverthwaite to the main road. There are bus stops on either side of the road, at the junction for Ulverston and Barrow with the Grange and Kendal stop across it by the station for the Lakeside and Haverthwaite Railway.

Haverthwaite lies on the bank of the River Leven, which drains water from Windermere and was once a part of the parish of Cartmel. St Anne's church, which was consecrated in 1838, was originally a chapelry under Colton.

The Lakeside and Haverthwaite Railway is all that is left of the line that ran from Ulverston to the south end of Windermere. Haverthwaite station was the main one on the line and had two platforms, trains being able to pass each other here. Besides passengers, the station was important for freight traffic. There was a narrow gauge line down from Low Wood gunpowder works taking sulphur and saltpetre from the station to the works and bringing back the finished product. The cotton mill and ironworks at Backbarrow were also served.

34. Walk 29 is met here.
35. Walk 30 uses a path to the left.

WALK 28

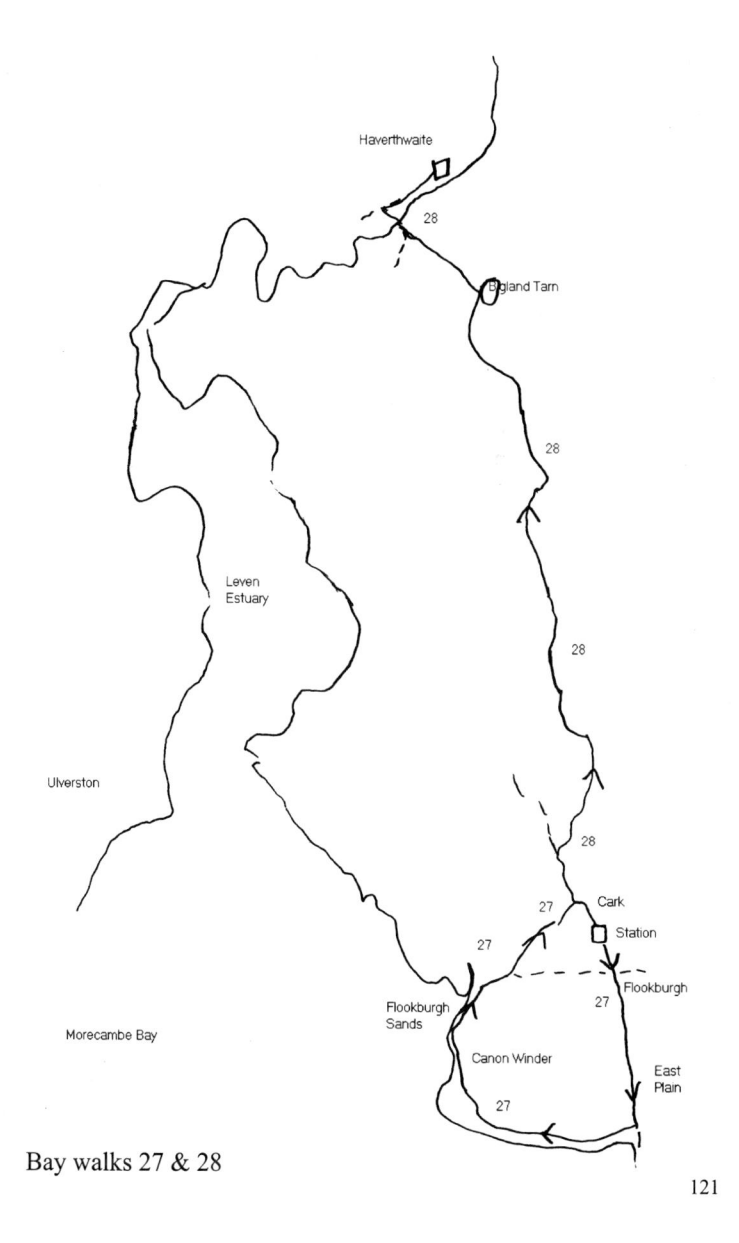

Bay walks 27 & 28

121

MORECAMBE BAY RAMBLES

WALK 29, HAVERTHWAITE, RUSLAND POOL, BACKBARROW, HAVERTHWAITE

Easy.
6¼ miles, 10 km.
Allow 4 to 4¼ hours.

A walk at the fringes of the Lake District that visits the industrial past.

Coming from the Barrow direction, at Haverthwaite station cross the main road and pass the bus stop from the Kendal direction to turn right down the minor road through Haverthwaite. At the Angler's Arms, take the road on the right to cross a stile by a gate blocking it; the road is a stretch of the former A590 from before the by-pass was built. Follow the old road, where nature is now taking over and come to a metal kissing gate by a field gate to pass through and then straight ahead along the field.

Bear left just beyond the narrow part of the field, passing by the wall on the left to come to a wooden stile. From there, follow the little lane beyond to a kissing gate out onto a road. Turn right along this road to go up to the A590. Cross over to the minor roads in front, using the island to the right for safety. Take the road to the right, also the A590's predecessor, and follow it to a junction where turn left.

At the next junction, go straight ahead (or continue along the road to the left to a junction and then turn right if the path about to be described is too muddy) by a County Council depot in a former quarry. Come to a field gate and follow the path along by the wall on the left, this being the part that can be very muddy. Keep on along the field, ignoring a gate on the way, and come to a wooden kissing gate to pass through. There, drop straight down the field with the wall on the right to come out onto a road and turn right.

Follow the road for about three quarters of a mile, passing Abbots Reading, to a junction at Ealinghearth and there take the road to the left for about a hundred and twenty-five metres to where there is a wooden field gate to go through. By the gate there is the path going down and to the left; it is followed along through marshy ground with trees in wetlands to the left. Go through a wooden kissing gate and then along the marshy ground in front. At the end of the trees on the left the path sets off over the open land in front, bearing to the left.

A stile is crossed onto the river embankment, Rusland Pool, which is still tidal at this point and up to the next bridge. Turn left along the embankment,

WALK 29

ignoring the path for Bouth across the footbridge. At some higher, rocky ground there is a stile to cross onto it and then drop down onto the embankment again.

There was another gunpowder works, Black Beck, near Bouth in the Rusland valley. A branch railway line ran along the far embankment of Rusland Pool to the works, which operated from 1862 until 1928.

Follow the path along, crossing stiles on the way, mainly on the top of the embankment preventing Rusland Pool and the tide flooding over the land to the left, but partly below it and slightly further inland. Come to a stile leading out onto the road at The Causeway, where to the right is a bridge over the river. Just before the bridge there is a stile on the left to cross and onto the embankment again. Keep on following the riverbank for around half a mile.

A stile leads out onto the A590, which is crossed with care, and then drop down to a stile back onto the riverbank on the far side. Follow the riverside path for a quarter of a mile and as the river swings to the right there is a ladder stile to the left by a small wooden footbridge over a dyke.

Cross the stile and follow the path as it bears right towards another stile to be seen by a gateway in front. Go through the gateway as the gate, at the time of writing, has not been used for years and continue along the path. Cross a stile and continue along close by woodland on the other side of a wall on the left. Some marshy ground is crossed using a stretch of causeway and then continue along with the fence over to the left. Keep going straight along and pass through a field gate in front, there is a waymarker. Once into the woodland turn right along the track until another is reached, where turn left along it to pass by the edge of the wood. This track is followed to houses at the beginning of Haverthwaite, where turn right onto a road.

Follow the road to the right, pass where there was the old railway bridge and come to a junction where take the road to the right; straight ahead is for Haverthwaite station. Cross the bridge (34) over the River Leven and at the road junction immediately beyond turn left; it is the road for the Crystal Engravers at Low Wood. Next pass an attractive little green and then, at the end of the houses, where the road starts to swing to the right, there is a bridleway to the left, leading into woodland.

The bridleway is followed, catching glimpses of the river that can be heard below to the left. Pass through a small wooden gate and continue on to a squeeze stile out onto a track above Backbarrow, it comes out onto a road where turn left and drop down to the village. On reaching the A590 turn right

MORECAMBE BAY RAMBLES

to the crossing and cross straight over with care and then drop down the cycleway in front, at the end of which turn left to pass the Whitewater complex. Cross the river and continue along the road to the left to Haverthwaite station about three quarters of a mile distant, where there is a bus stop by the station entrance for Windermere and Kendal buses and across the road for Ulverston and Barrow.

BWM29 Train and signal, Haverthwaite station.

The Whitewater complex at Backbarrow incorporates an old cotton mill that was notorious for its bad treatment of children in the early 1800's. Most of the children came from Liverpool, Whitechapel and Brighton. It is recorded that in 1816 hours were from 5 a.m. to 8 p.m. with a total of one hour for meals. On at least one occasion, when there was lack of work, the children were dismissed to fend for themselves and were expected to make their own way across the dangerous sands of Morecambe Bay. Later, the mill became an ultramarine works, the 'blue' being used in washing whites for a brighter appearance. At that time, many of the walls around the outside of the mill were covered in blue.

Backbarrow was home to one of the oldest continuously worked ironmaking sites in the country. There was a bloomery forge here in 1685 and a blast furnace was in operation from 1711. John Wilkinson, the ironmaster, received some of his early training at the works. Production did not cease until 1967.

34. Walk 28 is met here.

WALK 30

WALK 30, HAVERTHWAITE TO ULVERSTON

Easy.
9½ miles, 15¼ km.
Allow 4½ hours.

A very mixed walk involving estuary, villages and the industrial Ulverston Canal.

From Haverthwaite station cross the road and turn right down the minor road through Haverthwaite. At the Angler's Arms in front, take the road to the left. Come to a row of terraced houses on the left and at the end of them turn left along the path. Turn right to go along the bank of the river. At the road bridge (35) cross it and immediately after turn right onto the roadway, which is a private road but part of the Cumbria Coastal Way. This is followed to a wooden kissing gate on the right leading to a field by the riverbank.

Pass along the field and then through another wooden kissing gate to continue along by the river. Cross a small bridge by another kissing gate, over the following field, through yet another kissing gate and then over a bridge onto a roadway where turn right. This roadway leads down the River Leven, passing by Fish House Moss to the left, to Roudsea Wood Nature Reserve. All this area can be tidal; the day before this walk was done there had been a high tide and it was clear that water had flooded parts of the area. Note that permits are needed for entering the nature reserve apart from the rights of way.

BWM30 The Leven estuary and Greenodd.

MORECAMBE BAY RAMBLES

Continue along the roadway straight ahead, passing another footpath going to the right, and on leaving the woods see Greenodd ahead. Enter an open area with marshy ground on either side. As the road swings round to the left, pass over a stile by a field gate, cross straight over the field to another field gate at the end of that part of it, the field itself going on a lot further to the right. Once through the field gate and into the following field, cross over it by the fence on the right. A stile by a field gate leads out onto an embankment and from it continue along the grassy path in front, it leading to a large footbridge spanning the channel of the River Leven, and looking down Greenodd Sands, and then crossed to the main road in front.

Turn left along the road for a few metres and come to a path leading down and going under the road bridges, and then turn left along the path for Greenodd. On reaching the houses, turn right to go up the lane to the Ship Inn. From here, Greenodd can be explored, otherwise cross straight over the road at the junction and onto a very minor road to the left of the Inn.

Greenodd was a busy little port until 1869, exporting the slate, copper and lead from southern Lakeland. Greenodd and its neighbour, Penny Bridge, were both creek ports under Lancaster. Here was the highest point to which the River Leven was navigable. Now, there is no sign of Fell's Quay, Roper's Quay or Postlethwaite's Quay, the last traces of the port vanishing when the A590 was altered in the 1970's. The road alterations also took away the railway connection with Ulverston; the road using its trackbed and the bridge over the River Leven was demolished. A number of small ships were built at Greenodd during its time as a port and it had a sawmill.

Go straight up the road, passing the end of a footpath coming up from the road through the village and pass Egton with Newland Penny Bridge School. Continue straight up the road into Penny Bridge and turn left at the junction in front. Pass the church dedicated to St. Mary the Virgin, which has a fine Lych Gate in memory of the 1914-1918 War, and continue straight along the road for a little over a mile to Arrad Foot, where join another road and turn right.

On coming to the A590, turn right and cross it to the verge on the far side. Follow the verge, which is part of the Cumbria Way, for just over half a mile to the end of the dual carriageway, having passed a minor road off to the left on the way. Just after the end of the dual carriageway, turn down the road to the left, it being for Next Ness and Plumpton. Hoad Hill with its monument

WALK 30

on top is now quite close. However, the road is followed away from there, past a house, and at a junction just beyond turn left for Plumpton. Pass the houses at Moss Nook and then come to a bridge over the former railway trackbed for the line from Ulverston to Lakeside and then cross a bridge spanning the Furness line.

The road ends at Plumpton Hall and there continue ahead along the unsurfaced track leading out onto Plumpton Marsh where turn to the right and follow the path at its head. The path then drops down to go along the shingle at the head of the beach with Canal Foot at Ulverston seen ahead. The path is a mixture of shingle, sand and rock as it is followed along and can be very slippery; also, it is tidal. On reaching the houses at Canal Foot, turn up to the roadway by them and use it to the end of the canal.

Turn right along the canal towpath and follow it to its end, and come out onto the A590 again, where turn left. Go straight along the road, passing two roundabouts on the way, for the buses. For the station, go on a little further to some traffic lights and there turn left for a few hundred metres.

Ulverston was a place of sea trade, but had the problem of being well over a mile from the tides and the land in between being mosses. In 1760 the town had its own Customs House. A meeting in the Braddyll's Arms Inn on 8 August 1791 decided that the town should 'have a canal'. Shares were taken up and an Act of Parliament obtained. Many locally well known persons bought shares, including Wilson Braddyll of Conishead Priory and his wife. The Act determined that the canal should be built from Hammerside Hill (at Canal Foot) to Weint-end (Canal Head). The surveyor was John Rennie, one of whose other works was the Lancaster Canal.

The first sod was cut on 23 August 1793, a day of general holiday for the town. Work on the construction of the canal took longer than expected and it did not open until December 1796. At that time it was hailed as the shortest, broadest and deepest canal in Britain. It is only just over a mile long and has no bends in it from the former sea-lock all the way to Canal Head. At the top of its banks it is 65 feet wide and it is 15 feet deep.

Vessels of 350 tons were able to use the canal, increasing local exports of iron ore, iron goods, slates, bobbins and malt. Coal from south Lancashire and timber from Sweden were imported as was raw cotton for the spinning mills. Heavy horses towed them up the canal. The shipping trade peaked in 1846 with 944 vessels sailing in through the lock gates. Seventy years later trade on the canal ceased. The last vessel to sail through the lock gates was

MORECAMBE BAY RAMBLES

the 'Nebula' in 1949, from when they were concreted up. One vessel using the canal was the 'City of Liverpool' which was owned by the Ulverston ironworks.

The canal is now an enormous pond for the works of GlaxoSmithKline. The railway bridge into their factory remains although not now used by trains. It formerly carried the line from Plumpton Junction to Conishead Priory over the canal. The canal is popular with anglers and wildlife.

35. Walk 28 comes the other way across this bridge.

WALK 30

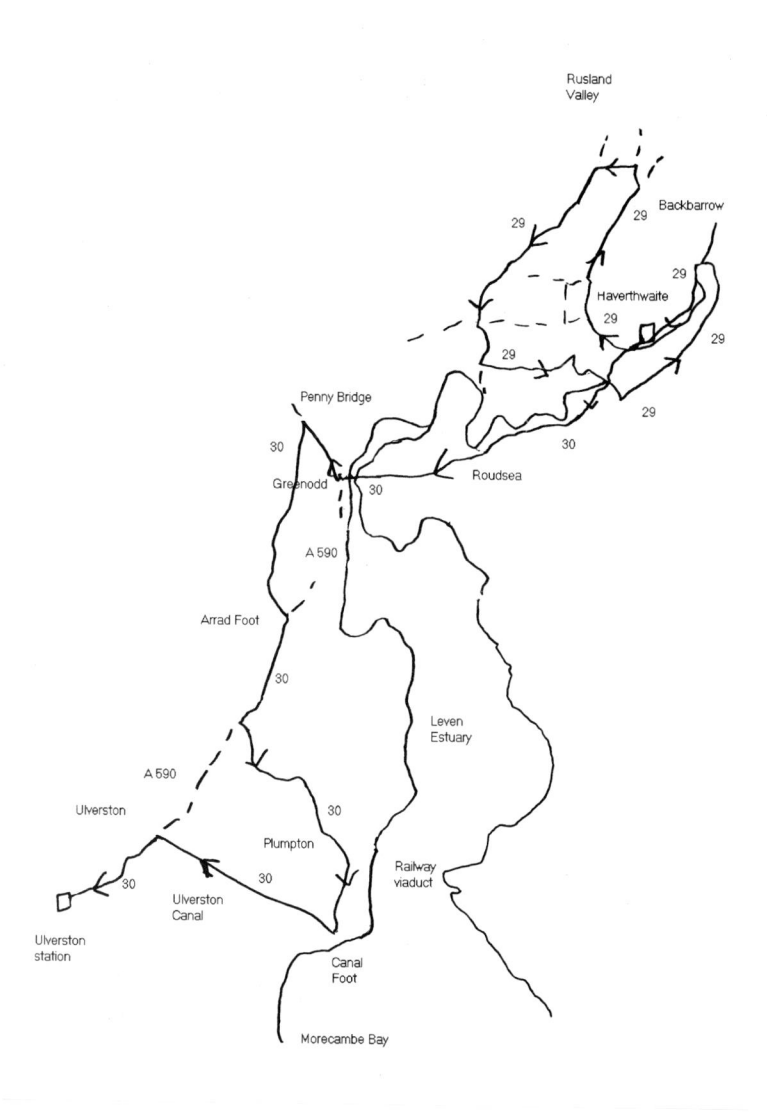

Bay walks 29 & 30

MORECAMBE BAY RAMBLES

WALK 31, ULVERSTON CIRCULAR VIA HOAD HILL

Easy.
4½ miles, 7¼ km.
Allow 2½ hours.

This popular short walk goes up the hill dominating Ulverston and provides good views of the town, the countryside and the Bay.

It was 1854 before the Furness Railway line from Barrow reached Ulverston although powers to build it had been received eight years earlier. The original station remains as a neighbour to the present one, but is now a car showroom. It had become a goods depot with the opening of the through line of the Ulverstone and Lancaster Railway. The present Italianate station was built in 1874, and has an unusual platform arrangement that was intended to facilitate the interchange of the Lakeside branch trains.

There was some shipbuilding in Ulverston. A major industry was the Ulverston Ironworks that was opened in 1874 and continued until the late 1940's, by when only one furnace was in use. The site was taken over by Glaxo pharmaceuticals.

Ulverston has had a Market Charter ever since the first one was granted by Edward I in 1280. It has both a daily covered market and an open air market on Thursdays and Saturdays, with stalls selling a wide range of goods and produce.

In 1764 Sir John Barrow was born in a cottage at Dragley Beck. He was educated at Town Bank Grammar School. He went on to become a seafaring explorer and discovered Point Barrow in Alaska. He had a forty years long career at the Admiralty, where he became 'the best Secretary of the Navy since Pepys'. Barrow was made a baronet for his services to his country in 1835. In May 1850, following Barrow's death

BWM31 Monument to Sir John Barrow, Hoad, Ulverston.

130

WALK 31

two years earlier, his two sons laid the foundation stone of the monument to their father, which stands on Hoad Hill. Hoad Monument is modelled on the lighthouse on Eddystone Rock and is built of limestone.

From the station, turn left to go straight down Princes Street, which changes to Queen Street and then becomes King Street at the top of Market Street. Pass along King Street to its end and then cross over to Church Walk. Hoad and its monument is seen straight in front. Go into the churchyard and turn right to pass in front of St Mary's Church, which is said to have been built in AD 1111, and continue along the path to a roadway. Follow the roadway straight ahead until coming to a metal kissing gate on the left leading onto the area of land in front of the John Barrow monument. A path, mainly tarred but the end part being grassy, winds its way to the top of the hill and the monument.

From the top, where there are very good views around, there is a grassy track going to the right towards the Leven Estuary. It is only a few metres before the track swings round to the left, away from the estuary, and is followed to a metal kissing gate by a field gate. Go through it and straight ahead to come out onto a minor road, Chittery Lane, where turn right. At the bottom, if time is short, turn left for the town. Otherwise, turn right and just after the last of the buildings on both sides of the road there is a metal kissing gate on the left, it being for Gilbanks.

Go through the kissing gate and along the grassy path, which turns left to continue along by the wall that had been being followed. As the wall goes over to the left, bear to the right to another wall. Pass round a disused metal kissing gate in a wall and follow the grassy path along by the wall on the left to another disused kissing gate. Continue near the wall on the left to a kissing gate leading out onto a minor road, which is crossed, and pass through another kissing gate.

Cross a stream, using a small concrete bridge, and then turn left. Follow the grassy path which is part of one ending of the Cumbria Way, pass a picnic area and enter a narrow stretch of woodland. On coming to a junction of paths it does not matter which one is taken as they meet up again. Go through a metal kissing gate and continue just above a Gill. The path comes out at an old area of Ulverston, The Gill, where the sculpture marking the southwestern end of the Cumbria Way is passed. After it, cross the road and bear down to the right. Pass straight along Upper Brook Street, passing the Laurel and Hardy Museum and out onto King Street, where turn right and follow the outward route in reverse to the station.

MORECAMBE BAY RAMBLES

WALK 32, ULVERSTON, BARDSEA, ULVERSTON

Easy.
7¾ miles, 12¼ km.
Allow 3¾ hours.

A walk leaving the town of Ulverston for the coast and then returning via a common and agricultural land.

Before the building of the coast road, the principle road from Ulverston to Barrow passed through Scales, Gleaston and Leece with branches to Baycliffe, Aldingham, Mote Hill and Roosebeck on the coastal side and Dendron on the inland side. People on foot could use the head of the beach, as with this and following walks.

On coming out of Ulverston railway station, turn left to the main road, which is crossed, and go straight down Conishead Road. Turn right at the next road junction and keep on along either Park Road or Victoria Road (which comes from the main bus stops) and they meet up again at a main road; John Barrow's house is less than 100 yards to the right. Cross that road to a footpath passing along by Dragley Beck. At the end of that path, do not cross the road bridge over the beck but, instead, turn onto the tarred path by it and continue to another road. Cross straight over the road and continue along the tarred path by the Beck to a further road and go straight along it.

The path by the Beck becomes very straight and is the remains of a historic ropewalk from the times when Ulverston shipping needed a supply of ropes. The Outcast ropewalk is 1282 feet in length. At the end of the footpath is the former Rope House, where there were offices and rope was stored. The ropeworks ceased to trade in the middle of the nineteenth century. But its site is still shown on the 1890 OS map.

The road crosses over the site of the former Outcast Bridge, which was 'abolished' in 1901. This road through from Hammerside Point to Ulverston centre was the route taken by people and coaches crossing the Sands to Flookburgh or Cark on their way to make the Bay crossing to Hest Bank.

Follow the road along and, just before reaching a junction by the main part of the GlaxoSmithKline factory, be sure to be on its right-hand side ready for a very minor road turning very hard to the right; it is part of the Cumbria

BWM32 Former works and the end of the Ropewalk, Ulverston.

Coastal Way. Go along it and in front of some houses and arrive at another road coming in from the right, the other end of which has been passed just before joining the Coastal Way. There, cross over diagonally to the right onto a no through road for Sandhall.

Pass Salt Cotes Farm and just after it, before reaching a junction for Sandhall, there is a metal kissing gate in the fence on the left. From it, bear to the right to go behind the trees at the back of Sandhall. Ahead, there is a field gate at the left-hand end of the trees with a stile to cross at its right. From there, continue along by the fence on the right, following the earthen track along.

Cross another stile by a field gate and pass between some farm buildings before coming out onto a roadway at a stile by another field gate where, just over to the right, there is a chimney standing on its own.

Keep straight ahead along the minor road to come out at the coast, close to where there was a level crossing over the old railway line to Conishead Priory. Turn right to follow the path close by the head of the beach; it comes to an end and then just walk along at the head of the beach. The Bay is quite

MORECAMBE BAY RAMBLES

broad here, looking across to Heysham Power Stations. To the right are paths into the grounds of Conishead Priory.

Although there are no rights of way through the grounds of Conishead Priory, walking along many of the paths is permitted and the building is often open in an afternoon, but check locally for times.

In the 12th century, Gabriel de Pennington, with the encouragement of William de Lancaster who was Baron of Kendal, erected and endowed a hospital for the poor and decrepit at Conishead. This was given to the charge of Augustinian monks. It was not long after its foundation that the hospital was elevated to priory status, but had to maintain its charitable foundation. Following the dissolution of the monasteries it was largely dismantled before falling into the hands of a local squire. Later, the Bradyll family, who did much rebuilding work before becoming bankrupt, acquired it. Now it is a Buddhist retreat and temple and much further restoration work has been done. Crossing the sands of Morecambe Bay would be familiar to the monks, the Priory paying the salary of the Levens Sands guide.

The track goes to the right on reaching some woodland to pass along its edge rather than at the head of the beach, which is only a few metres to the left. The woodland comes to an end and the path continues along with a fence on the right and the beach on the left. The spire of Bardsea church comes into view ahead. The end of a minor road is passed before continuing along with a fence on the right. It is all part of a sea defence area. At the time of writing, it had been badly damaged by a storm.

Walk along the grassy path at the edge of a field that is entered, keeping the fence on the left. After this, continue along the track above the wall on the left. By the 'Kingfisher' premises, come to the end of a road, cross over it and over a wooden stile in front. Cross to the fence in front and follow it along, the original line of the path having been badly damaged so as not to be safe to follow. At the end, cross over a stile onto the proper path just above the beach and follow it along close to the sea defences.

On reaching the main road, keep on along the beach until where cars park and there leave the beach, cross the road and then go straight up the one in front. Come to a junction where turn right to Bardsea village. At the beginning of the main village street at the *Braddylls Arms* (36), where there are bus stops, turn left down a minor road, if not first looking around Bardsea village.

Mannex directory of 1851 shows that a steam packet service from Fleetwood brought passengers across Morecambe Bay to Bardsea five times a week and there was a weekly service to Liverpool.

By the beach is the much altered building that was the local mill, now a cafe. It ground corn until the 1920's.

Storey Bros. Ltd. was once a major Lancaster employer. The founding brothers were two of the sons of Isaac Storey, who was born in Urswick in 1798. He should have taken holy orders, but married, raised a family, and entered the teaching profession, and is listed as the schoolmaster at Bardsea in Baines's Lancashire of 1824. In 1835, on a wild autumn day, the family left Bardsea to cross Morecambe Bay to Lancaster. In due course, William set up in business and Thomas joined him. Storey Brothers manufactured table baize or oilcloth, of which they became major manufacturers.

Another brother was John, who when aged about twelve, went out on surveys with Jonathan Binns, and who was probably the only other professional person in Bardsea at the time. Binns had done a survey and proposed the building of a railway line from around Heysham, across Morecambe Bay to near Bardsea.

Bardsea church was erected in 1848. Colonel Bradyll of Conishead Priory was a main instigator of it being built, but his bankruptcy in the middle of proceedings led to problems. Monies were raised by public subscription for its completion. In the end, the Reverend Petty, the son of a rich local landowner became the principle benefactor and also its first curate.

On Birkrigg Common, above Bardsea, are old homesteads and burial sites. There is also a concentric stone circle, known as the Druids' Circle, which is late Neolithic. It is of two concentric stone rings, making it fairly unusual. The inner ring is the more conspicuous and has a diameter of 8.5 metres, and is free from bracken. The outer ring of about 20 stones is 24 metres diameter and many of them are often covered by bracken.

A junction is shortly reached and there turn right to go up the road to Bardsea Green. At the end of the houses the road becomes a track and at its end there is a wooden gate leading out onto Birkrigg Common. There are views of both Morecambe Bay and Ulverston up here. There are many paths over Birkrigg Common (37). For this walk, go straight ahead from the gate. Come to where you can go down to a cattle grid to the right, but continue along the path a little further to where it swings right down to the road. Turn left along the road and come to two signposts for footpaths. Turn right down the grassy path towards an outer corner of a field below and on reaching it go down the

MORECAMBE BAY RAMBLES

grassy track with the wall on the right and a field gate in front. As will be appreciated when on the Common, there are various paths which lead down to here, and the essential thing is to reach this spot.

Cross over a stile by the field gate and onto a good grassy roadway. Follow it to its end at a tarred road and there turn right for a few metres. On the left is the entrance to Middle Mount Barrow and just to the right of it there is a metal kissing gate to go through. Pass straight along the driveway towards the field gate in front and there go through the small iron gate to its right. Turn right to follow the lane round the farm buildings and then continue along the lane to The Grange, the next buildings on the right, where turn down the path to the right. The path comes out at a roadway which is crossed and then go a few metres down the road in front before turning left to the main road. Turn right down the main road and in about a mile reach Ulverston station.

36. Walk 32 uses this stretch of road as well until reaching Bardsea Common.
37. Walk 32 leaves here.

WALK 33

WALK 33, BARDSEA, ALDINGHAM, GREAT URSWICK, ULVERSTON

Easy, but with rather slow beach walking.
8½ miles, 13½ km.
Allow 5½ hours.

A walk that is a mixture of beach and limestone country.

There are two pairs of bus stops in Bardsea and either can be used. Go through the village and to the left at the *Braddylls Arms*. At a fork in the road, take the turning to the left to drop down to the coast. Cross the coast road and the car parking area and turn right at the head of the beach. On the way along, it will be seen how the high tides can cause erosion of the bank above the beach, causing some fencing to hang loose.

Pass by some chalets on the right and cross a major stream. (By the chalets is a roadway from the beach which is a way up to Baycliff.) A number of tractors and trailers used by fishermen out on the Bay are passed as you continue along the beach until Aldingham church is reached up above. At the far end of the church is the way up from the beach, which is left to go straight up the road ahead. At the main road a quarter of a mile away, cross over to go up the minor road in front to Scales about a mile further on.

BWM33 Scales Green.

It is said that St Cuthbert's church once stood in the middle of the village of Aldingham, but that erosion washed away the buildings below it. Traditionally, the monks carrying the body of St Cuthbert in the ninth century, to avoid desecration by the Danish invaders, rested here. Unfortunately, no remains of a Saxon church have been found, the present building dating from around 1147. The first rector in 1180 was Daniel, possibly the son of Michael le Fleming.

The Norman le Flemings lived at the Mote, a motte structure that has now been partly eroded by the sea. Below it is an ancient square moat, which is not directly connected with the motte, with Moat Farm by it.

Baines, in 1824, shows that the parish of Aldingham included the townships of Aldingham Lower, Aldingham Upper, Gleaston and Leece, and had a population of 760 in 1821. One of the people he lists as living in Aldingham was the Rev John Stonard, DD, who was very wealthy and paid for the wall protecting the graveyard from the sea. He also built the former Rectory, which stands by the church.

Scales has just one street forming the village and forms part of the parish of Aldingham. The name comes from the Old Norse for a hut or huts on a hill. George Patrickson, who was born in Scales, became wealthy and returned to the village on the death of his father. He then ran an old malt kiln to provide work for some local people.

Limestone was burnt at Scales and there is an old limekiln on a path towards the coast, quite close to Scales Green.

On reaching Scales, follow a road off to the right for about fifty metres and there, just as a bend in the road is reached, a bridleway for Sunbrick goes off to the left. Follow the good clear track along, going through two pairs of metal field gates on the way. Come out into a little lane (38) and cross the small stone step stile through the wall in front. Bear about 45 degrees left in the field towards where a corner of the field in front juts out and come to a length of farm track in front of it. (Close by to the left is the old settlement of Foula.) Follow the farm track to the left for a few metres and see a stone step stile into the field in front.

In the field, bear a little under 45 degrees to the left and come to a track dropping down to a field gate. Drop down part way towards it and then see a wooden stile about twenty-five to thirty metres to the right of the gate. Cross the stile and go along by the hedge on the left; it is a mixture of hedge and fence as it is followed and then becomes a wall, the path running quite close by it. Ignore a path going off up to the right, but keep down at the bottom and see a house in front.

Go over a stone slab stile and down into the garden of the house, pass along the very left-hand edge of the lawn, and down to the road. Turn right along the road. On reaching a road junction, take the minor road to the left, with a good view of Urswick Tarn.

Great Urswick used to be called Much Urswick. The village encircles the tarn, which is inhabited by waterfowl. Around are the remains of ancient settlements. Foula has been claimed to be late Iron Age, but is now thought to also have Roman connections. On Skelmore Heads are the remains of an early earthwork that was probably a hillfort.

Urswick is believed to have the oldest Christian foundation in Low Furness. The church, which is dedicated to St Mary and St Michael, is situated between Great and Little Urswick. The tower has walls 1.5 metres thick at the base and a lack of windows, suggestive of fortified church towers of the 14th and 15th centuries. Within is a part of a Saxon cross with a runic inscription and two carved figures. It appears to date from the 7th century. The church also has a three deck pulpit.

Roman finds have been made around Urswick. Some dressed sandstone to be found in various walls of this limestone region are thought to be from an early Roman fort.

There are two pubs in Great Urswick. The Derby Arms is named after the former powerful landowner of the area. General Burgoyne was defeated at Saratoga by General Gates in 1777. One story about the General Burgoyne is that it was so named by one of his troopers on returning home after the American Wars of Independence.

Pass a kissing gate on the left (39) and then come out into Great Urswick. Turn left along the road for about seventy metres to where there is a track to the right between two of the houses. Turn up this track, which is part of the Cistercian Way. At two metal field gates side by side across the track, go through the left-hand gate and along by the wall on the left.

The wall shortly comes to an end and from there continue walking straight on ahead over the grassy field in front. Pass below what is the site of the ancient hill fort at Skelmore Heads to the left and by a field wall on the right. Go through a metal field gate and continue along by the wall on the right. At the corner of the field cross a stile and drop down to the corner of two other fields, which meet here. Pass straight across for a few metres and on the left,

MORECAMBE BAY RAMBLES

just past the entrances to two fields, there is a stone stile to be crossed. From the stile, go along by the wall on the left to come to another stile onto a little lane leading to a road.

Cross the road diagonally left to the road for Ulverston; it is followed and joined by another road coming in from the left. On reaching a crossroads, turn left down Swarthmoor Hall Lane. As this road bends round to the left, see the Hall on the right. Pass the entrance and then on the right there is a lane going behind the Hall to follow. The route is very clear as it goes through two kissing gates, over a small stretch of field, through another wooden gate that leads over a bridge spanning a stream and then continue along the main path. This comes out onto a road where turn left for two hundred metres for Ulverston station.

Swarthmoor Hall was built around 1586 and was the home of Judge Fell and his wife, Elizabeth in 1652. George Fox, visited the Fells and Mrs Fell became a convert to Quakerism. In 1699, eleven years after the death of the Judge, Fox married his widow. The Hall later left Quaker ownership but was purchased by the Society of Friends in the 1950's and is now in regular use. It is sometimes open to the public.

38. Walk 33 uses this lane on the way to Dalton.
39. Walk 36 uses this gate.

WALK 33

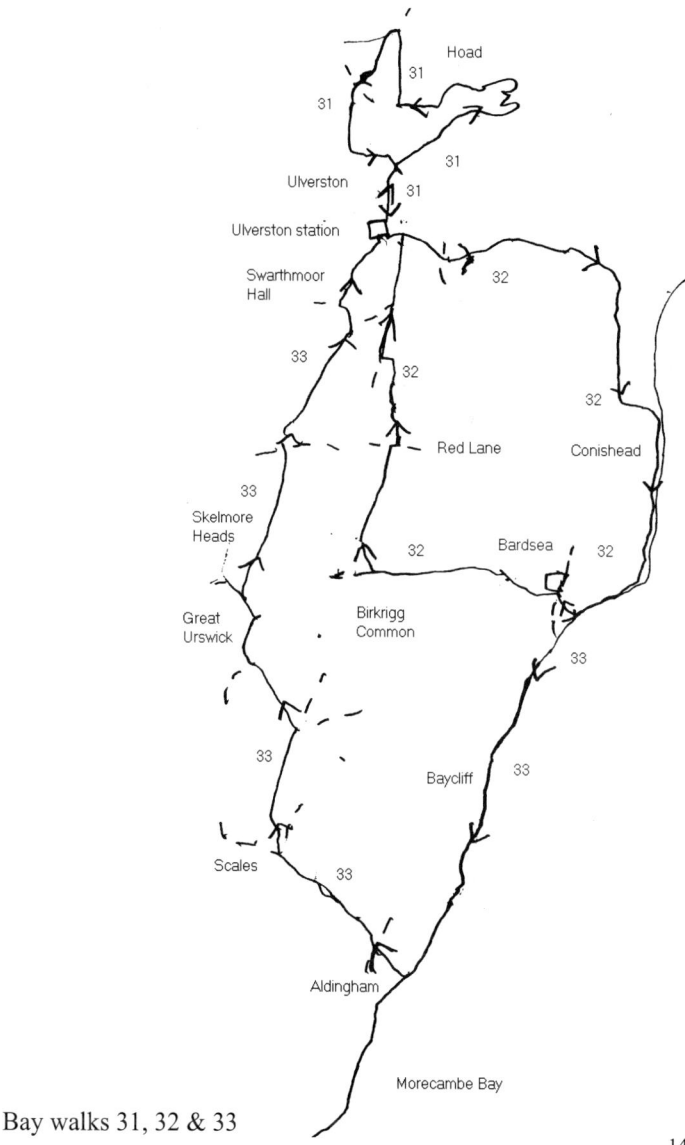

Bay walks 31, 32 & 33

MORECAMBE BAY RAMBLES

WALK 34, BARDSEA, BAYCLIFF, LITTLE URSWICK, DALTON-IN-FURNESS

Easy.
7½ miles, 12 km.
Allow 5 hours.

A walk with a mix of limestone country and agricultural land.

Starting from by the Bradylls Arms in Bardsea, turn right down the minor road and at the next junction turn right to Bardsea Green. At the end of the houses the road becomes a track, which is followed to a gate after which turn left (36) going up the path over Birkrigg Common, passing through bracken, and quite close to a wall on the left. At a quite close junction continue along the path on the left; there are good views of Morecambe Bay up here.

At the next junction, take the path straight ahead, ignoring the one going to the left and next come to a crossroads of paths where continue straight ahead towards Sunbrick, the hamlet to be seen ahead. Cross over another path and then at the following junction, take the more minor path to the left, going down towards the road at Sunbrick. (By going further to the left across Birkrigg Common, the stone circle can be passed. It is then necessary to turn right along the road to Sunbrick.)

On leaving the path, go straight ahead down the road and come to a metal field gate in front. From it, follow the track in front, passing some of the houses of Sunbrick on the right. Continue straight along Sunbrick Lane, it becoming a path between two hedges. It comes out onto a broad farm track to follow down to a tarred road and there drop down amongst some of the houses of Baycliff to come out on to the village green. (At the end of The Green there is a path to the left going down to the main road and the bus stops.)

A road down to the beach at Baycliff is the way that iron ore was taken to the beach, from where it was loaded onto flat-bottomed boats that floated off at the next high tide. The ore was taken to local furnaces and some as far away as Wales. At the foot of the lane was an office for recording cartloads.

Baycliff was a strongly Quaker village and suffered persecution because of this.

WALK 34

BWM34 Baycliff.

At the far end of the Green, take the road going upwards to the right; it narrows and then broadens again. Notice two stiles of drystone walling on going up the road, the one on the left being quite different from the one on the right. Pass a very large limekiln close to Baycliff Haggs Quarry. On coming to a road crossing at the top, turn right along it and in about half a mile there is a farm track going off to the left to be followed to a stone stile in the wall at its end (38).

Cross the stile into the field and then pass straight up it, bearing towards the mixed boundary on the left. On reaching the boundary, continue along by it, seeing Little Urswick straight in front. Pass through a stile by a field gate into the next field and again continue by the hedge on the left until towards the end of the field where bear a little to the right of the boundary to go to a metal kissing gate. The following field is crossed towards the left-hand side of the hedge seen in front and there go through a stone squeeze stile at the very edge of the hedge and then turn right for about thirty metres to a metal kissing gate.

Turn left once through the kissing gate and go down by the wall on the left. At the end of this narrow field, come out onto a road at a field gate and turn right. In about seventy-five metres there is a broad field track going ahead as the road turns right. By it there is another path going straight up a narrow field, across a track and through a farmyard at the top. A personal preference is to use the good track to the right and come out by Urswick Village Hall. There, turn left to go through the village and come to a shelter by the village green. (The other path comes out here.)

Little Urswick has below it the remains of a medieval field system.

Excavations were carried out at Urswick Stone Walls in April 1906. In the centre of the walls are the remains of a large circular hut of nearly 12 metres diameter. There were at least five roundhouses on the site. It is not certain how old the walls are, but it is now considered that they may be part of a Romano-British settlement. The builders of the walls made use of the natural configuration of the site. A late Celtic bronze fragment was found near the hut-circle.

By the shelter, there is a signpost, turn right to follow the track which passes between two of the houses and then through a wooden kissing gate. Follow the grassy path along as it goes towards the limestone crags in front. Cross a wooden ladder stile and then continue following the path up the crag, going a little to the left. From up there, Morecambe Bay can be seen in the distance. Continue following the grassy path to a stone squeeze stile to pass through and then turn along the grassy path to the left.

Another stone squeeze stile in the field wall is passed through and then go straight across this next field to a very large field gate on the far side; it leads out onto a track where turn right. Cross the stile at the end of the track and then go over a very narrow piece of field to another stile by a field gate. The next field is crossed quite close to the hedge on the left. Go a little to the right as you drop down towards then end of the field to come to a tight squeeze stile leading out onto a road.

Cross the road to another squeeze stile and then cross straight over the field and then through another squeeze stile out onto a road. (At the time of writing, this squeeze stile and hedge were so tight that it was better not to cross that field but to turn right along the road to a nearby junction and then turn left again.) On the opposite side of the road is the footpath for Standing Tarn and Dalton, but there is much more room to cross this squeeze stile, which is by a field gate.

Go along the field by the hedge on the right and at the end there is a stile to cross into the following field. The path goes straight over the field, which is a large one. Assuming it is there, Standing Tarn will come into view on the right, but it is a Tarn that completely vanishes in drier weather, leaving its site visible on the right. When full of water, it covers quite a large area. If the correct line has been taken across the field, a stone squeeze stile is reached leading into the following field. Go to the left over this field but so as to gradually approach the hedge in front that then becomes on your right.

At the end of the field, by a field gate there is a squeeze stile leading onto a roadway. Turn right along it for a few metres to another squeeze stile on the left and go through it to pass straight down the field by the hedge on the right; as it is descended there is a good view of Dalton-in-Furness in front. A wooden stile is crossed at the end of the field, leading onto a grassy lane which is followed along, passing some houses and then under the railway line. Follow the road from there up to the main road in Dalton-in-Furness to Tudor Square, where there are the bus stops, or continue on for about another two hundred and fifty metres for a road to the left leading down to the station.

Dalton was the ancient capital of Furness. Ulverston, Barrow and Walney were once parts of the parish, which at one time also included Hawkshead and up to the top of Lake Windermere.

The castle is a simple keep that was erected during the reign of Edward III by the Abbots of Furness as a defence for the nearby Furness Abbey, this following Scottish raids. It is probable that there was some earlier form of building on the site housing the local Court Leet for Plain Furness. Courts were held on the first floor of the Castle, the courtroom being reached by means of a spiral staircase. Criminal cases would also be held here as well and it was a prison until 1774. It is not known whether or not there were other buildings attached to the keep, perhaps accommodation for a gaoler.

In front of the castle are the fish stones and market cross that were erected in 1869. The stocks and whipping post along with the covered market hall are long since gone. The original Market Charter was granted by Edward III, but it has long since lapsed in favour of Ulverston.

By the castle stands St Mary's church standing immediately above the slope of a hill. A church stood here before the erection of Furness Abbey and it was from then that parts of the parish were transferred from the vicar to the control of the Abbot. A document in Barrow Record Office shows that in 1869 "His Grace the Duke of Devonshire being the Lay Victor, is obliged to supply the Vicar with ten gallons of wine for Easter day and to pay £17-6-8 to him as Vicar in lieu of the tithes of the whole parish". The same document also reveals that several worshippers absented themselves if there was a collection!

Before the development of the mining industry, Dalton was a single street, Market Street, running down from the castle to Tudor Square, which was then named Bally Green. The second half of the 19th century saw a very rapid expansion of the population with rows of terraced housing being built for the miners.

The railway came to Dalton in 1846 when it was a terminus of the Furness Railway. It was to be another eight years before the line was extended to Ulverston.

36. Walk 32 uses the road to here, but then continues straight ahead over the Common.

38. Walk 33 crosses the track.

WALK 35

WALK 35, ALDINGHAM, GLEASTON, NEWTON, DALTON-IN-FURNESS

Easy.
5½ miles, 8½ km.
Allow 3½ hours.

A walk involving limestone country, agricultural land and a historic watermill with perhaps castle ruins as well.

Starting from the bus stops at the Ulverston end of Aldingham, turn down the road to the church where, turn right along the road and follow it to the main road again. Here are the bus stops for the Barrow end of the village. Cross straight over the road to go through a squeeze stile into a field. Go up the field by the hedge on the right. At its end a stream causes a wet patch as the stile is crossed into the following field. Continue along by the hedge on the right.

On reaching the next fence, instead of going through the gateway, turn left up the field, strictly by the field boundary, but in reality a bit further in as is dictated by the wetness of the ground. Continue up the field to its top right-hand corner where there is a stone squeeze stile which is not seen until it is reached owing to its being at right angles to the hedge. When in the following field, bear right across it to a small bridge leading through the hedge and fence and into the following field.

Once in this field, turn to the left to go straight up the hillside towards its top, looking back to Aldingham and Morecambe Bay on the way. At the top there is a short stretch of wall amongst the hedge. To the left of it there is a squeeze stile leading into the following field. Go up the field by the mixture of hedge and wall on the right. At the top there is a stone squeeze stile followed immediately by a wooden stile into the following field. There continue along by the hedge on the right to a wooden stile followed by a stone squeeze stile into the following field.

This field, which is part of Beacon Hill, is in two levels, an old boundary having been removed to make it one field. Go up and over the top of the field by the upper edge of the lower level and, as it is crossed, Gleaston Mill comes into view below with Gleaston beyond. On reaching the hedge at the bottom of the field, turn right. At the end of the field there is a lane to follow as it drops down towards a road, coming out at a field gate. There, turn left for Gleaston Mill, but you may want first to turn right for the farm seen a short way ahead and by which are the ruins of Gleaston Castle, returning the same way. In total, with a good look at the castle ruins, the diversion is no more than half a mile.

The now ruinous Gleaston Castle was home to the Harringtons. There are two claims as to when the castle was built. One is that the Saxon Lords of Aldingham moved here in the 13th century after their land was washed away at Aldingham, but the other is that they built the castle after the raid of Robert the Bruce in 1322. There is no conventional keep to the castle, but it had a tower at each corner. It is said to have been sold to the City of London in 1652.

Further down the valley from the castle is Gleaston Mill, operated by water that has flowed from Urswick Tarn. It is now a working museum, having earlier bean closed. The wheel is an overshot breast wheel.

Gleaston village is named after the Saxon 'farm by the smooth river', Gleaston Beck.

BWM33 Gleaston Mill.

WALK 35

Pass Gleaston Mill and, on entering Gleaston village, continue straight ahead past the houses of Mill Lane, leaving the road going on to the left. Next, go along the main street to come to crossroads where cross over to a rather steeply rising road in front, it being for Dendron and Dalton. Follow the road and then, as it drops down again and turns left for Dendron, go through the field gate on the right. Pass by the hedge on the left and just after the entrance to a field there is a stile on the left leading into it. Cross over to the far left corner of the field and go through the field gate into the following field. Cross it towards the road up the hillside in front. On reaching the hedge at the far side of the field there is a squeeze stile to cross and then use the stepping-stones over a small stream and go up to the road.

Walk straight up the road, which turns to the right and then, a few metres after passing a metal field gate on the left, there is a metal kissing gate to go through. Cross straight over the field. From the hedge on the far side, turn right for a few metres to another metal kissing gate into the following field. Go along to the hedge in front and then turn left to go up by that hedge, following an earthen farm track. Newton is seen in front and to the right on reaching the top of the field,

The farm track comes out at a field gate and once through it bear to the right. Go across the corner of the field to a squeeze stile by a wooden stile about 45 degrees to the right. Cross the next field more or less straight across to where a gap in the hedge in front is seen, this being where there is a squeeze stile into the following field. From that stile, bear a little to the right to another field and cross it, still 45 degrees to the right, to a wooden stile in the fence in front, which is just to the left of a field gate.

Once over the stile, turn 45 degrees to the left to the next wooden stile in the hedge in front. From there, bear over to the right and at the end of the field cross a wooden stile to drop down to a road, where turn left into Newton (39). A few metres along the road there is a track going off to the right. Go up this track and as it turns right after about half a mile cross the stile straight in front. Cross the clear path straight over three fields to Dalton-in-Furness.

Newton means 'New Town' in Old English. It was a granary to the nearby Furness Abbey.

On coming out onto a road, cross straight over it to a footpath between the houses. Follow this path straight along, passing through three wooden kissing gates and at the last of them come out onto a road. Turn left along the road to its end and then turn right. As this road is followed, bus stops for Barrow

MORECAMBE BAY RAMBLES

and Ulverston buses are passed. At the end of the road, turn left along the main road, Greystone Lane and follow it along to the bridge over the railway line. There, drop down to the appropriate platform if catching the train. For the town centre of Dalton-in-Furness, continue straight on along the road.

39. By going through Newton to the main road and a few metres to the right there is a path across a field to meet walk 38 to Furness Abbey.

WALK 36

WALK 36, ALDINGHAM, NEWBIGGIN, LEECE, RAMPSIDE

Moderate.
7 miles, 11¼ km.
Allow 4 hours.

Walk along the coast and then turn to go through farmland and visit Leece village built round a pond before returning to the coast again.

From the bus stops at the Ulverston end of Aldingham, turn down the road for the church, pass it and go down to the beach where turn right. Keep on walking along the head of the beach, which is a bit rough in parts. On coming to a green cabin on the right there is a diversion that can be done; a signpost indicates the path.

BWM36 St Cuthbert's Church, Aldingham.

For the diversion to Moat Farm, cross the stile to the right of the cabin and then go diagonally right across the field to another stile in the hedge on the far side. Keep on following this diagonal line across the fields until reaching

151

MORECAMBE BAY RAMBLES

a stile in the far right corner of the last one and come out on to the road. Turn right for a little over a hundred metres to see the ancient moat to the right, by Moat Farm. Return to the beach by the outward route.

To resume the main walk, go along at the head of the beach again or use the path from by the chalet, which is easy going. The grassy path is followed to come out at two tracks side by side. As this is a coastal walk, take the left-hand one and shortly come out onto the A5087 at Newbiggin. There, turn left for about fifty metres to the bus stops and a road to the right leading into the village. Go up the road to its end at a farm-yard and there turn left to go through a part of the yard and then along a farm track, with some of the farm buildings to the right.

Newbiggin is a hamlet within Aldingham. Its name is from the Old English for 'new building'. The 1840 6 inch Ordnance Survey map shows that it then had a smithy and a malt kiln with a limekiln by the shore.

Follow the track along, pass through the gate at its end, and continue down the field by the hedge at the right. Cross the ditch in the bottom right corner of the field and go up to the corner of the fence by the sewage works, where cross the stile. Continue down by the sewage works fence, across the works entrance and to a wooden stile in front. A wooden footbridge is then crossed, spanning Deep Meadow Beck. From the bridge, turn right to go along by the Beck until coming close to a small footbridge where turn to the left and cross the field.

The field is quite level apart from a slope upwards at it far end. At the bottom of that slope there is a squeeze stile into the following field. Once in that next field, turn right up the slope for a short distance to a wooden stile in the hedge, which can be seen from the earlier stile. The wooden stile crosses barbed wire, and leads to a slate squeeze stile into the following field. Cross this field down the middle; it is not an evenly shaped field, the left half going further ahead than the right. There is a field gate with a wooden stile by it to cross at the left-hand end of the shorter right-hand half of the field. Pass along this next field by the hedge on the left.

At the end of the field there is a field gate leading out onto a track, from which go through the gate a few metres to the right and then along the field by the hedge on the left. It turns round a corner and comes to a wooden stile which is crossed. Turn right for about fifty metres to a chained barrier between two posts, its guarding a wooden stile into the following field, where go along by the hedge on the left. Keep following the hedge until the far

WALK 36

right corner of the field can be seen and there turn towards it and go out at a gate leading into Bracken Bed Lane.

On the opposite side of the lane there are three field gates in a row, the middle one being the one to use. Pass straight up the field and as it is ascended Leece comes into view a short way ahead. The field is oddly shaped with a number of corners to the right. Go ahead to an inward jutting corner with a part of the field going further ahead to its left. At that corner there is a squeeze stile into the following field where pass along by the hedge on the left; at its end there is a stile in the hedge leading to a little lane that drops down to the road by Leece Tarn. Many waterfowl inhabit the tarn.

The Domesday Book refers to both Leece and Another Leece. The name refers to a pasture in Old English or to a place lower than some neighbouring place. The lands were given to Michael le Fleming by Henry I.

Leece was subject to an agreement between the Abbot of Furness and le Fleming that both could hunt over the territories of it, Dendron and Stainton, without detriment to the warren of the owners. The agreement did not include farm servants of the Abbey.

Before a new chapel was built at Dendron in 1642, the people of Leece had to go four miles each way to worship at St Cuthbert's church at Aldingham.

In order that most of Leece village can be visited, turn right along the road and at the junction, turn left and again at the following junction. On going down this road, still close to the Tarn, come to a very minor road to the right, a sign indicating that it is to Moss House, a quarter of a mile distant; it is part of the Cistercian Way. On reaching the house at the road's end, go straight ahead, over a wooden stile by a field gate and drop straight down the farm track and into the field at the bottom. There, bear left to a wooden footbridge that can be seen on the far side.

Once over the footbridge, bear left over the grassy path up the field to the gate to be seen in front; it is by a signpost. Go through the field gate onto the Roosebeck path and on reaching the buildings of Moss Side, pass through the field gate on the left, by the buildings, and come to another field gate to use. From it, turn left to another field gate, pass through it and go along by the fence on the left. As the fence goes further over to the left, follow the earthen path as it goes round by the hedge on the right to come to a small wooden footbridge in the corner of the field.

Cross the footbridge and the stile by it and then go diagonally to the right over the field to a stile in the hedge opposite. The stile leads onto a minor

MORECAMBE BAY RAMBLES

track where turn left to come to a large field gate leading out onto a tarred roadway. Turn right along that roadway, passing Newtown, and come to a road junction. It is a staggered junction, where the road that is nearly straight ahead is taken and followed to Rampside church at its end.

At the right of the church there is a wooden stile leading into a field. Turn right up the field to the gate at its end, but do not go through it. Turn left along the fence to where it ends at a hedge. There, cross a stile into the field to the right, where turn left to follow the hedge, passing through a metal kissing gate on the way. Pass a stile to the left, its being for another path to Rampside. There is a wooden stile to cross where the fence starts to turn diagonally right. Cross the stile and continue along by the same fence but on its other side towards the field gates to be seen ahead.

At the gates, go through the kissing gate to the left, it leads onto a track (40). Follow the track to the left, it having fences or hedges on its sides and continue straight on ahead to a field gate leading out onto the road at Rampside. The bus stops for Barrow and Ulverston are to the right, by and opposite the Village Hall.

In 1797 Rampside was an excellent place for sea-bathing. In the early 1900's people came by train from Barrow to Rampside for a day out.

Rampside Hall was built sometime between 1580 and 1600. The building is topped by a row of twelve chimneys which are known as 'The Twelve Apostles'. In the 1700's the land behind was woodland where now there are only fields.

In February 1865 Rampside had an earthquake. William Parker of the then Bay Horse Inn (now the Concle Inn) and John Thompson, a fisherman, were walking from Foulney to the Roa Island causeway when ahead of them they saw a mass of sand, stones and water thrown into the air. On returning to Rampside they found that many of the houses were damaged; there were cracks in the west wall of the hall.

St Michael's Church stands uphill outside the main village. Although it was not erected until 1840, it is believed to have been built on the site of an old burial barrow. It is known as the 'seamen's church' owing to the number of mariners buried there.

40. Walk 38 uses this track in reverse.

WALK 37

WALK 37, DALTON-IN-FURNESS, LINDAL, URSWICK, DALTON-IN-FURNESS

Easy.
9 miles, 14¼ km.
Allow 5 hours.

Visit a small town and two villages together with an ancient and fascinating church.

From Dalton station go up the road to the town centre and turn right along the main street to Tudor Square, where there are bus stops. There, take the road to the left, signposted for the Wildlife Park. Go straight up the road, passing other streets on the way. Cross the bridge over the by-pass and immediately on the right is the road up to the Wildlife Park, its also being a public footpath. On reaching the car park bear over to the left to where an earthen footpath is to be seen going into some trees. Go up the path, cross two stiles in quick succession and then follow the path along by the hedge on the right, on the far side of which are some of the inhabitants of the Park.

BWM37 Baboons look at the snow, South Lakes Wild Animal Park, Dalton.

MORECAMBE BAY RAMBLES

A stretch of what is clearly an old sunken roadway with banks to the left and right is followed, but this soon ends with there then being just a fence to the right. Another wooden stile is crossed. The path then comes out into an open area before coming to a wooden ladder stile leading into the field to the right. Cross the field by the fence on the left until a wooden stile is reached to re-enter the field you were in previously. Continue along the field to a ladder stile to the left of a field gate and cross it out onto a road where turn left to the junction ahead and there turn right for Lindal in Furness, three quarters of a mile away.

There is no record of Lindal in Furness until 1220 when it was listed as a Grange to Furness Abbey. A tarn formerly occupied the centre of the village, where there is now a Green, and its waters turned red from washing the wheels of carts used in the transport of haematite ore.

Much ore from Lindal was transported by railway and there were extensive sidings. On 22 September 1892 a steam locomotive fell through a hole created by mining subsidence and is still there. Fortunately, the crew jumped clear.

The road passes St. Peter's, the parish church, on its way to The Green. Either turn right or go round The Green, if wanting to see more of Lindal, and come to the busy A590. Cross it at the pedestrian crossing and then go straight down London Road. Cross the railway bridge and come to the candle factory from which a lovely scent fills the air. A public footpath crosses the car park, with the factory on the left. At the end of the car park a metal field gate leads into a field.

Go up the field by the hedge on the left until reaching a kissing gate by a field gate. Once through it pass down that field by the hedge on the right. At the bottom of the field, go through another kissing gate and immediately turn right to the hedge at the bottom of the field, where turn left. On reaching a metal kissing gate by a field gate, go through it and bear diagonally left across the field to where there is a short stretch of fencing as opposed to hedging. By it there is another kissing gate into the next field, which is crossed diagonally left to the far left corner and out onto a road. This is a meeting place of three roads and three footpaths.

Cross over the road into the field in front and there go along by an old boundary hedge on the left, its shortly becoming a fence. On reaching a hedge a little further on, cross the wooden stile and then drop down the stones into the field below. Cross diagonally right for a few metres to pass through

WALK 37

a metal kissing gate. From there, go up the slope and cross the stile at the top. The field is crossed by bearing a little to the left so as to come to a wooden stile in the fence in front; it is roughly half way along the width of the field. From it, go along by the remains of an old wall on the right. Keep on down the field, passing the possible site of an old burial chamber over to the right.

At the end of this field, cross over a stone step stile into the following field and continue down it by the wall on the right. As the wall bears off to the right, follow the grassy path going ahead and a little to the left towards the houses of Great Urswick. At the end of the field there is a squeeze stile by a field gate leading out onto a lane which comes to a roadway leading to the main road through Great Urswick. Turn left along it to the road junction by the pub and restaurant, where turn right. Follow the road round, perhaps diverting down to Urswick Tarn on the way, and at the junction ahead (41), turn right to continue past houses bordering the Tarn.

Shortly after passing the last of the houses, there is a kissing gate on the right. Go through it and straight across the field to another kissing gate on the far side of which a plank bridge takes the path across a stream. Pass close to the bottom of the tarn and then turn to the left towards another footbridge spanning the Tarn's outlet. From the bridge, go straight up by the ditch until, just to the right of the church, there is an entrance into the churchyard. Turn left past the church to a small metal kissing gate leading out into a field.

Cross the field to its far left corner and there go through another metal kissing gate into the following field and immediately turn right to go along by the hedge. At the end of the field a kissing gate leads out onto the road by Urswick village hall. Turn left along the road and go into Little Urswick.

Close to the beginning of the village there is a footpath to the right for Dimple Holes Lane. Turn up it, the first part being a track, and then go through a field gate. Follow the grassy path by lines of stones and bushes towards a wall in front. Before reaching the wall, bear over to the right so as to follow the wall round a corner. At the end of that wall there is a wall in front which is crossed by a wooden box stile. Cross over the following field to another wooden box stile in front, its leading into woodland.

Follow the woodland path, it going a little to the left, and then leave the woodland at an ordinary stile. Just after leaving it, over to the left, is the site of an old settlement, Urswick Stone Walls. Once over the stile from the wood, bear over to the right and keep on going over the lower part of the field and come to a stone step stile leading over the wall in front and onto a lane that is inclined to be muddy.

Turn left along the lane, follow it round a corner to the right and through to its end at a road, where turn left. A junction is reached in just over 300 metres with a road going to the right and a fork seen 100 metres ahead (42). Turn onto the road going to the right, its actually leading to Lindal. At the next crossroads, turn left for Dalton-in-Furness. On the way along, Standing Tarn may be seen over the hedge on the left, assuming that it is not dry. The road comes out at a junction where turn left for the bus stops at Tudor Square and for the railway station which is reached by turning left by Barclays Bank.

An alternative ending to this walk from Little Urswick is to first pass through the village, passing the shelter and bus stop, and coming to a minor road to the right. Take that road, pass a path on the right and then one on the left. The road starts to swing round to the left and there is a signpost by the stile into the field. Go ahead and a little to the left to pass to the left of three trees seen in front and continue on to what is the far left corner of the field.

Go through the field gate and then through the right-hand field gate of two straight in front. Pass along the track, at first by a hedge on the left and then over open field. As the track is followed, it starts to bear to the left and become rather indistinct, but it is slightly raised from the part of the field to its left. A kissing gate in the wall in front is reached and then a very narrow section of the following field is crossed to a stile to the right of a field gate and out onto a road.

About twenty metres to the right, there is a stone squeeze stile on the far side of the road. There, bear over to the right and follow the track along just below the fence bounding Stainton Quarries. The path turns to the right to go over some limestone and then becomes a grassy path over the field. On reaching the boundary in front, turn left to go by it and at the end pass through a stone squeeze stile into the next field. Continue straight along by the fence and hedge on the left, at the other side of which is the very large quarry, which is still in use. At the very end there is a wooden stile leading out onto a lane with another squeeze stile in front. Cross the field straight towards the two pylons seen by the farm in front and at its end stiles lead out onto a road.

Cross the road to a stile and then go up the field a little to the left to cross another stile. Bear to the right over the following field to another stile. Once over it, go down the field by the electric fence on the left to a field gate at the bottom. On leaving the gate, turn right along the farm track. Follow the track and come to some steps up to the left leading to a wooden stile to cross. This is just after passing some structures connected with the farm.

Pass an indicator showing a route bearing right (it leads to Standing Tarn), but go straight ahead, crossing an embankment and going beneath a pylon

WALK 37

line, to the left-hand corner of the field, only a short way ahead. There, cross a wooden stile into a field in front and go along by the wall on the left; it is just below an old railway track from Stainton Quarries to Dalton.

Follow the path along the field, its bearing round to the right and come to a wooden stile by a field gate in a fence in front. Cross it and bear over to the left towards the houses. Pass through a metal kissing gate by a field gate and go along the road roughly straight in front, Cantabank. Drop down the road and at the end come to the bridge by Dalton-in-Furness station. Also, there are bus stops close by both to the left and to the right for buses to Barrow and to Ulverston. Continue along the road past the station for the town centre.

39. Walk 33 passes this gate.
41. Walk 33 uses the path to the left about 70 metres before the junction to Ulverston.
42. Walk 34 to Dalton can be used from just beyond the junction seen ahead by using the road to the right up to the footpath.

MORECAMBE BAY RAMBLES

WALK 38, BARROW-IN-FURNESS, FURNESS ABBEY, DALTON-IN-FURNESS

Easy
7¾ miles, 12 1/2 km.
Allow 3½ hours.

Leave the town of Barrow-in-Furness for the remains of a Cistercian Abbey and visit a town that protected the abbey.

BWM38 Furness Abbey.

Barrow-in-Furness did not exist until the middle of the nineteenth century. In Baines's Lancashire of 1824 it is just mentioned as a hamlet in Dalton parish. It was just a small group of agricultural dwellings, but the coming of the railways and the haematite ore industry changed all that. In 1846 the Furness Railway opened its line from Kirkby and Crooklands to Barrow and Rampside. The railway transported ore and slate for shipping out of Furness by sea. Four piers were built and Walney Channel dredged.

Henry W Schneider, a speculator and iron dealer, discovered a large and rich iron ore deposit near Askam. Schneider & Hannay had the first iron blast furnace built at Hindpool. It was built by Josiah Smith and said to be the finest in the country. Barrow-in-Furness then started to grow rapidly.

In 1864 a steel company was formed by James Ramsden, who was the managing director of the Furness Railway, to build a works using Sir Henry Bessemer's manufacturing process. Later, this works merged with that of Schneider & Hannay to become Barrow Haematite Steel Company. By 1876 it was the largest steelworks in the world, when sixteen blast furnaces were in production. In 1983 the Barrow Steelworks Ltd,. then owned by British Steel, ceased production. Now, it has all gone and only the old slagheaps are left to be seen.

Devonshire Dock Hall dominates Barrow. Submarines are built within its walls. Shipbuilding in Barrow started in 1847 when William Ashburner, formerly of Ulverston, established a yard where Devonshire Dock now stands.

In 1863 James Ramsden advised the Duke of Devonshire, a local landowner, to purchase Barrow Island from T Y P Michaelson for the Furness Railway Company. The Island became the centre of the dock system and the shipbuilding industry. It is enclosed by Ramsden Dock, Buccleugh Dock and Devonshire Dock.

As Barrow became affluent, it was decided that a new Town Hall was needed. It is Victorian Gothic in design. Work was begun in 1882, but was not completed until October 1886. It was officially opened on 14 July 1887, the year of Queen Victoria's Golden Jubilee, by the Marquis of Hartington, the future 8th Duke of Devonshire. The local story that it was erected back to front is untrue, it is just that the rear entrance was used more often as a matter of convenience.

Barrow is one of the earliest planned towns anywhere in the world. Many of the streets were planned to accommodate large numbers of often single men employed in the iron and steel industry or in the shipbuilding industry. In 1874 the 'Scotch' tenements were built on Barrow Island using the plans for the Gorbals tenements in Glasgow.

Both merchant and naval ships were built in the shipyards. Submarines are still built in Devonshire Dock Hall. In its shadow is the Dock Museum, close by which were the original houses of Barrow, where there are models of a number of these ships plus other records. Within is the Victorian graving dock, which is Grade II listed.

The shipbuilding industry led to Barrow being very badly bombed during the Second World War when 618 houses were destroyed and 10,563 were damaged out of a total of 18,000.

MORECAMBE BAY RAMBLES

With the loss or reduction of its old industries, Barrow-in-Furness is turning to a new industry, one that would never have been envisaged by Ramsden, Schneider and the other industrialists who founded the town—tourism. It is hoped to redevelop part of the old industrial area and dock system to a marina.

From Barrow railway station entrance, turn left for Abbey Road, which leads towards the centre of the town. Cross over Abbey Road and go straight along Rawlinson Street in front. Cross a number of minor streets and a major road on the way to its far end at another major road where turn left. Go along this road, Salthouse Road becoming Roose Road after passing under a railway bridge, and up to a pedestrian crossing. There, cross the road and turn left for a few metres to the next turning on the right. Pass right down the road to its end and then turn left.

At the next junction there is an unsurfaced track going off to the right and this is the route to follow. Pass beneath the railway again and once under it turn left to follow the track at the back of an old industrial area by Cavendish Dock, which is now a reservoir. Keep straight on ahead until a junction is reached with the main track leading to industrial buildings, another track to its right (43), and to the left, by the security fence, there is a path. Follow the path, over a stile, and turn left in the field, passing above the security fence.

On reaching a fence at the top of the field, turn right to follow it, looking back over the docks and tidal area to Walney Island. As the end of the field is approached, Rampside Road comes into view below and it is joined by crossing a wooden stile. Turn right along the road to a farm on the left and there cross over to go along the minor road in front, Dungeon Lane.

Today, it is hard to believe that the rural hamlet of Stank was once an important haematite mining area. A railway line ran from Salthouse Junction at Barrow through to the mines. The line ran via Roose Cottages to the mine and remains of the track and the site of a bridge crossing the road are still to be seen.

On coming to a crossroads, go straight over and onto Stank Lane. On the left, particularly just before reaching the hamlet of Stank, the remains on an old railway line are to be seen. Pass through Stank and the site of a now demolished railway bridge over the road. As the road rises and starts to bend to the right, see on the left a kissing gate leading onto a path for Newton.

Go up the field bearing diagonally right towards the fence and the far right

WALK 38

corner. There, cross a wooden stile into the next field, where turn right. Up here is an old mining area. At first, the path is of red earth and then becomes a rather vague grassy field path as it goes to the left of some former pits. It drops down and round a lot of gorse to a wooden stile in the fence ahead. Cross the stile and then pass straight along the following field by the hedge and fence on the right.

In about a hundred metres there is a crossroads of paths (39) by a field gate with an adjacent kissing gate. Here, turn left and on dropping down the field a stretch of road comes into view. Go through the metal kissing gate out on to the road and turn left along the road for about two hundred metres where, as the road goes left, there is a kissing gate to the right, by a sign for Bow Bridge.

Bow Bridge was built in the late 15th century and must have seen many monks and lay brothers cross it on their way to Furness Abbey. It had been allowed to become covered in growth before restoration about 1970.

Tucked in the "glen of deadly nightshade" are the ruins of the Cistercian Abbey that was once second only to Fountains Abbey for that Order. Furness Abbey was founded in 1127 by a group of monks from Savigny in France. It once had lands in Ireland and the Isle of Man as well as in many parts of Cumbria and other places.

The Abbey had fishing rights around the region and also across Morecambe Bay where it owned the Beaumont fishery near Lancaster.

It was following the settlement of the monks at the Abbey that Furness began to be developed. Agriculture improved and knowledge and religion were advanced. The only person more powerful than the Abbot of Furness was the Monarch.

In April 1537 the Abbey was surrendered to the king. This was a blow to local agriculture, no longer were there the large demands for provisions. Now, the Furness Abbey ruins are under the care of English Heritage.

Cross the bridge and turn right to follow the path beneath the railway. On coming to a concrete bridge, cross it and keep straight on by the stream, but on its other bank. At the end of the field there is a kissing gate leading along to the gate by the railway line. Cross the railway with care to come to the road circling Furness Abbey. Turn left to follow it round it to the abbey entrance.

A few metres after leaving the last of the ruined buildings associated with Furness Abbey, there is a footpath going straight ahead as the road

MORECAMBE BAY RAMBLES

swings to the left. Follow it, beneath the railway line and then along by its side, along the Vale of Nightshade. In season, there are some delicious blackberries down here.

Come out onto a road, which is crossed, and then drop straight down onto the track on the far side, which is also a cycleway. Pass beneath the railway line again and go through the metal kissing gate into a field. There, turn left so as to go over to the woodland on the far side of the field, crossing a stream on the way. By the woodland there is a kissing gate, but do not go through it. Instead, turn right to follow the grassy path towards some trees, its going close by the stream which had been crossed.

Pass beneath the railway line that avoids Barrow on the way up the Cumbria Coast and follow the path along with the stream below. The streetlights and the first houses of Dalton-in-Furness come into view. At the end of the path, go through a large metal field gate and onto a tarred roadway and pass the Green Area of Dalton.

Shortly before reaching the main road, turn left to go up by the church, passing along Church Street. Pass St Mary's and then along Market Place to the right of Dalton Castle. Drop straight down Market Street to the centre of Dalton and then turn right by Barclays Bank to follow the road round for the railway station on the right, passing bus stops for Ulverston or Barrow on the way.

39. Walk 35 comes to Newton and can be linked by using the path to the right.
43. Walk 39 uses the track to the right.

WALK 39

WALK 39, ROOSE OR BARROW-IN-FURNESS, ROA ISLAND, BARROW-IN-FURNESS

Easy.
9¼ miles, 14 km.
Allow 4 hours.

Follow a former railway line that is now partly a nature trail and visit Roa Island, which was once a railway terminus and port.

From Barrow station, follow the route as per walk 38 to where the track splits at the entrance to industrial buildings.

Roose is a suburb of Barrow. The name refers to a moor or heath. The 1890 OS map shows just a few dwellings there besides Roose House, the Ship Inn and Roose Farm. Oddly, a milepost showing it was 27 miles to Carnforth is also shown.

BWM39 Boats by the causeway to Roa Island.

MORECAMBE BAY RAMBLES

From Roose railway station either cross the bridge when coming from Barrow or turn right towards the main road when coming from the Ulverston direction. Turn left down the main road to come to a roundabout. At it, cross over to go along Rampside Road. At a junction, either go straight ahead down Rampside Road or follow the minor road, Old Rampside Road until the two meet up again. A few metres beyond the junction, there is a footpath sign by a wooden stile on the right (44) leading into a field. Go up the field by the fence on the right. Shortly, the dock area and Walney Channel come into view.

On reaching the end of the field, turn left and follow the fence down. Towards the end of the field there is a wooden stile on the right to cross and onto a roadway. Cross over the roadway to the further track to the left (43) and turn down it. Follow the track along, passing the gas terminals on the way. This is part of both the Cumbria Coastal Way and the Cistercian Way and is part of a former railway line. To the right is Roosecote Sands.

At the end of a long, straight stretch, the track swings round to the right, continuing to follow the coast round Westfield Point. Roa Island and Piel Castle beyond come into view. Shortly after that, the track leaves the shore and goes a little further inland, after which it turns back again to the right. Next, some houses of Rampside are reached and the path comes out onto a road, where turn right for Roa Island. Cross the causeway onto Roa Island and go straight up the street to the end. There, from by the Lifeboat Station, is the jetty from which the ferry sails to Piel Island, half a mile distant across the channel. Return is, of course, by the same route.

Banker John Abel Smith purchased Roa Island in 1840 in anticipation of its future development and he sold out to the Furness Railway in 1853. The causeway from Rampside was built in 1847.

A single-track railway line ran across the causeway to Piel Station on Roa Island. Its terminus was by Roa Island Hotel, which was built as Piel Pier Hotel, but is now closed.

A large pier jutted out into the tidal channel, known as Piel Harbour, from by the station. The original pier was opened in 1846 and replaced in 1868, but it fell out of use in 1894 and was demolished. Oddly, there are no known photographs of either pier. Passenger steamer services from Fleetwood, Belfast and the Isle of Man once used the pier.

A small ferry, sailing from a slip by the Barrow lifeboat station at the end of the island, serves Piel Island. The castle on Piel, which was known as

WALK 39

Fouldrey Castle or The Pile of Fouldrey, was built to protect the harbour and Furness Abbey from the sea and particularly from Scottish raids. In 1327, during the reign of Edward III, a licence was granted to crenellate the building. The castle was in poor condition by the time of the dissolution of the abbey. Now, people often visit the ruins in the summer months, when they also visit the pub, the landlord of which is known as 'The King of Piel'. Piel Island is owned by Barrow Corporation and it is they who approve who becomes the 'King'. At the time of writing, the Ship Inn is closed for renovations, but it is hoped to be open for the 2008 season.

At Rampside, turn right along the road, passing two sets of bus stops, and by the Village Hall there is a footpath to the left for Westfield Nature Trail. Turn left along the farm track passing the backs of some of the houses of Rampside. Pass through a gateway and the track bears to the right, going between a fence and a hedge. Pass round some bushes at a rather tight corner and continue along the very clear path to come to a wooden kissing gate by a signpost, where go straight ahead (40). Follow the broad track with fences on either side, seeing the gas terminals to the left. Pass through a wooden kissing gate and the path continues straight ahead, the farm track going to the right. Pass a viewpoint and then come to some steps down to a roadway for the Gas Terminal. Cross straight over it to go through a wooden kissing gate and continue along the path.

For all of it being so close to the Gas Terminal, the Nature Trail has a variety of flowers around here and, as the area is marshy, there are dragonflies and damselflies to be seen at the right season. A footbridge is crossed over some of the marshy land. The path then drops down to another one, where turn right. A marshy area is passed on the left, which is occupied by waterfowl. The path comes out at a wooden kissing gate onto the former railway track used on the outward journey, and turn right for Barrow.

Follow the track straight along, passing the path used from Roose, and then along the unsurfaced roadway, going straight across the middle of an empty area. On coming to a tarred roadway, turn right, go under the railway line and up to the road in front, where turn left. Follow the road along, beneath a railway bridge and continue straight along it. For Rawlinson Street, the quickest way to the railway station, its end which is across to the right, is reached shortly before coming to a church.

On reaching a major junction, take the road to the right, using the pedestrian crossing to do so. Go onto Duke Street and follow it along, pass

MORECAMBE BAY RAMBLES

the Town Hall, which is the terminus for a number of bus services, and at the next roundabout, Ramsden Square, turn right up Abbey Road for the railway station.

40. Walk 36 uses this track in reverse.
43. It is here that walk 38 is met.
44. Walk 38 is met at this stile, but going in the opposite direction.

WALK 40, WALNEY

Easy.
Part 1, 6 miles, 9½ km.
Part 2, 5 miles, 8 km.
Allow up to 4½ hours for the two parts combined.

The walk is in two parts that can be done separately or together. Much of it involves the use of roads as there are not many paths on the island, which is long and narrow. The first part of the walk covers the very end of Morecambe Bay whilst the second part is strictly just beyond, but is a very nice walk. The whole is very adaptable according to time available.

Walney is separated from the mainland by a narrow channel and was reached by a number of fords. From 1878, following dredging to make a harbour at Barrow losing two of the fords, a ferry crossed over to Vickerstown. It was replaced by Victoria Bridge (Jubilee Bridge from 1935) in 1908, which was a toll bridge until 1935.

BWM40 Biggar Dyke.

MORECAMBE BAY RAMBLES

Walney is a long but narrow island. It was well known to the monks of Furness Abbey, who it is believed obtained food from here. They helped to maintain the ancient Biggar Dyke, protecting the eastern shore from the tides, and the flat top acted as a road.

Biggar is named from the Norse meaning "barley field". The small village is clustered on a hillock at the end of the dyke. The people of Biggar used Biggar Bank, on the seaward shore of Walney, as grazing land until it was bought by Barrow Borough Council and formally opened by Alderman Fell on Good Friday 1883 for use as a recreation ground.

North Scale is an ancient village and it will be seen that some of the buildings are a lot older than those of Barrow. In 1644, during the Civil War, most of the inhabitants of the village were roundheads. It was attacked by the Royalists and put to the torch.

Vickerstown started to develop from 1899 when Vickers bought the Isle of Walney Estate Co and started the building of housing for its workers.

From Barrow railway station, turn down Abbey Road, on its far side, towards the town centre, perhaps going down to Ramsden Square and turning left along Duke Street to the Town Hall. On the way there are bus stops and at one of these catch a bus for South Walney or Biggar Bank.

At South Walney the bus leaves the streets and turns right with a wide expanse of saltmarsh on the left. Here, at a shelter, is the bus terminus. From it, walk the few metres ahead to the main road and turn left along it. Stops for the Biggar Bank bus service are passed. At a junction to the left there is a signpost indicating that the road is for Biggar and South Walney Nature Reserve, which is five miles distant. Turn down this road with the saltmarsh over on the left.

Shortly, it will be noticed that there is an embankment between the road and the saltmarsh. This is the start of the ancient Biggar Dyke. Only a few hundred metres before reaching Biggar Village it will be noticed that there is a way over the top of the Dyke. By crossing it, good views can be had along it in both directions on the seaward side.

Continue straight on along the road past Biggar and in about half a mile come to a wide saltmarsh area with Roa Island and Piel Island to be seen beyond. On reaching a track going to the right between stone walling, ignore it but continue for about another hundred metres to a lay-by and a track going to the right. A signpost indicates that it is Honeypot Lane. Turn along the lane to its end, which is only five minutes walk, and come out onto a beach. Here, look across to distant Fleetwood towards the left. Ahead are to be seen the rigs of Morecambe Bay Gas Field and the offshore wind turbines. From here, return to the road.

Those walkers wanting to visit the South Walney Nature Reserve should continue straight along the road to the right for about three miles to its end, but it is likely that most people going to the Reserve will go by car as it is a ten mile return walk from South Walney plus distance walked at the Reserve. Otherwise return by the outward route to Biggar village. There, take the road to the left until it bends to the right at a car park. Go onto the car park and turn right along the path by the shore for Sandy Gap, two kilometres distant. Follow the gravely path along Biggar Bank until The Roundhouse is reached and turn right for the bus stops. Otherwise continue on with the second part of the Walney walk, which is joined here.

Again starting from the South Walney bus terminus, go ahead to the main road and turn left to follow it to its end at The Roundhouse. An ending at the coast on Walney is perhaps a fitting terminus for the A590. Drop down to the left of The Roundhouse onto the path seen below, it crossing the grass above the beach below Biggar Bank. Turn right along the path and at the junction immediately in front take the path to the left, which is followed to its end at Sandy Gap, half a kilometre distant.

At Sandy Gap, cross over the road that ends there and onto a tarred walkway above the beach and by the fence bordering the golf course. (If coming from Biggar and there is not time for the longer walk, go straight along the road, passing the end of the Biggar Bank road, and on starting to drop down from the highest point see Devonshire Dock Hall in front and drop down to Jubilee Bridge.) Follow this path straight ahead, it becoming untarred further on, close to the head of the beach. Pass another path to the right before coming to a fence with an opening onto the golf course. Do not enter the golf course, but either follow the path along the beach or the very narrow path at the top of the sea defences. A good track above sea defences is then followed to the end of the road at West Shore.

At West Shore, turn right along the road and about 100 metres from where it turns right there is a minor road to the left, Cows Tarn Lane. Follow this lane along; it goes to the left at a junction just ahead. The end of the lane is at North Scales, where turn right along the road and pass some older buildings. The road comes to the promenade along by Walney Channel and is followed to Jubilee Bridge seen ahead, the only bridge crossing to Walney.

Cross over Jubilee Bridge and either go through the gardens on the left or continue to the road junction ahead and turn left. Pass Devonshire Dock Hall and come to the Dock Museum. There, cross over the road from Walney and

MORECAMBE BAY RAMBLES

then the road immediately to the left, using the pedestrian crossings. Drop down the path by a brick wall and straight along to a main road junction ahead. (There may be changes to the roads and crossings in 2008 when Ironworks Road will become part of the A590 along with Walney Road.) There, turn right up to the main junction ahead where turn left, having first crossed the pedestrian crossing shortly before the junction. Abbey Road is followed straight ahead, passing the roundabout at Ramsden Square and crossing at a pedestrian crossing by the library. Continue straight along Abbey Road to the railway station.

WALK 40

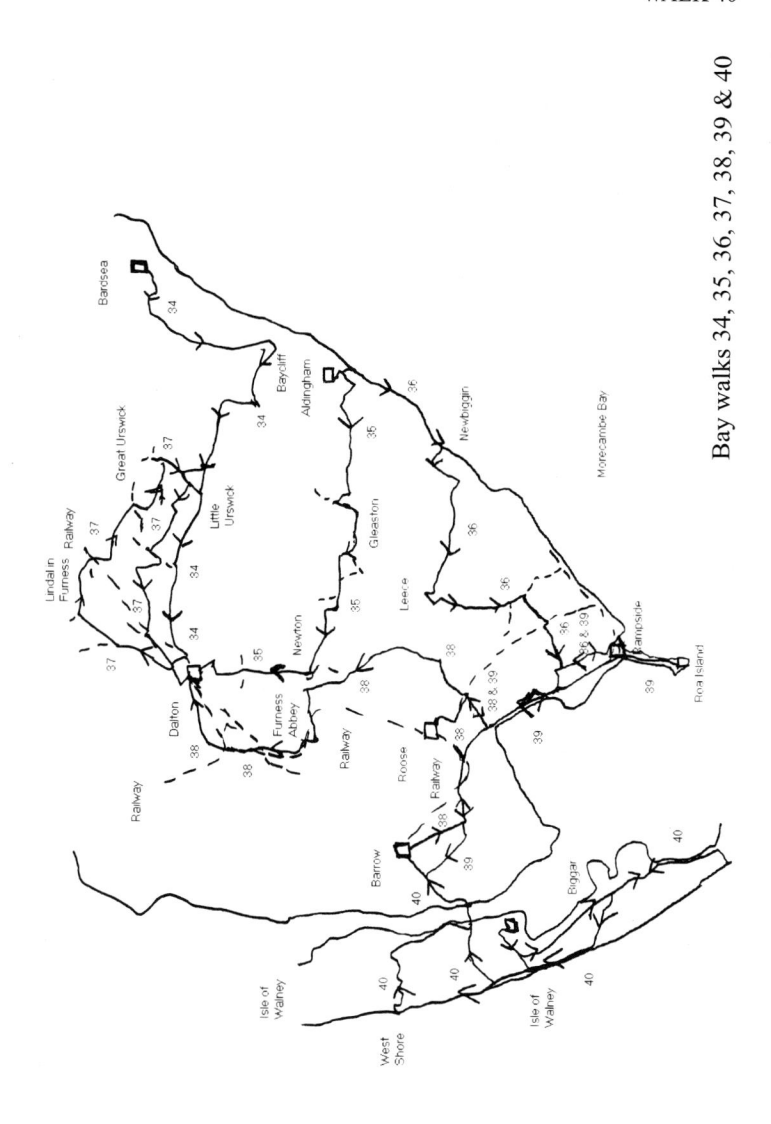

Bay walks 34, 35, 36, 37, 38, 39 & 40

MORECAMBE BAY RAMBLES

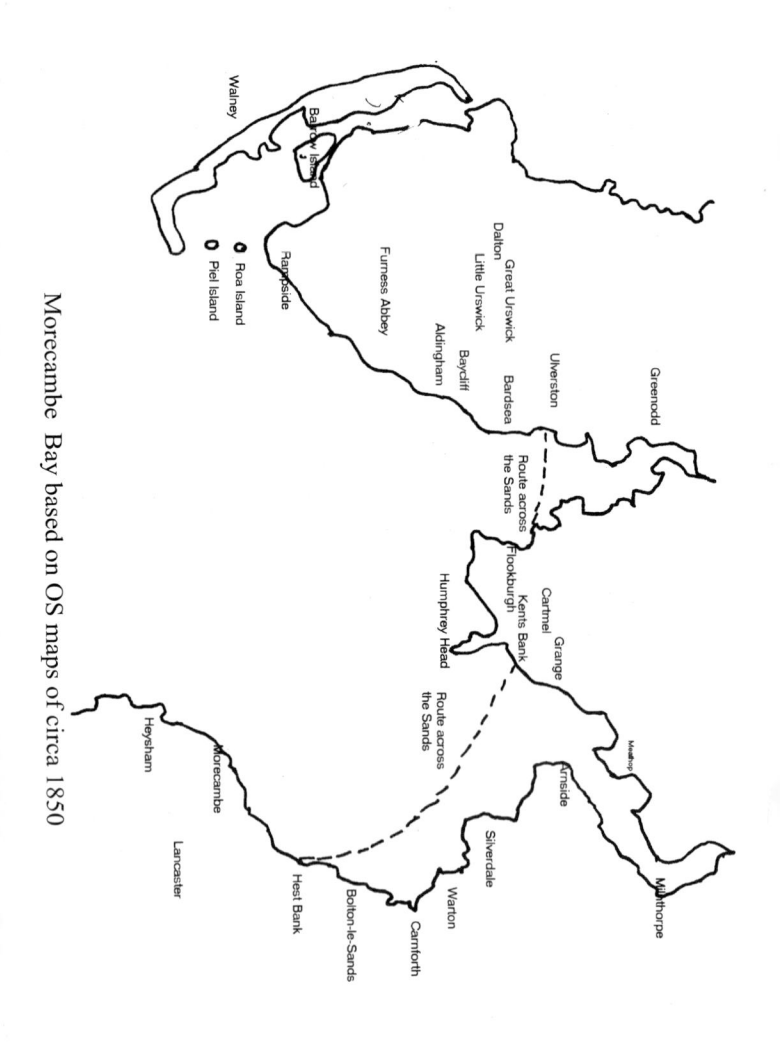

Prints from illustrations in this book.

Photographic colour prints of any of the plates used in this book can be purchased from David Farnell Photographic Laboratory Ltd., 26 Lakes Enterprise Park, Caton Road, Lancaster, LA1 3NX, 01524 847647. Please contact them for prices and sizes, stating that they are required for prints from Yan Press books.

55 555 Walks. Robert Swain.
Yan Press ISBN 0-9540713-0-1.

Explore the countryside, towns and villages between Lancaster and Keswick. These 55 walks are a mix of both linear and circular walks and are very adaptable to the needs of the walker. They include everything from the simplicity of walking along the towpath of the Lancaster Canal, through visiting Lakeland valleys, such as the Kentmere Valley, to climbing some of the Lakeland peaks under 2,000 feet, such as Walla Crag and High Tove. A brief history of the many places visited is given.

Available from good bookshops and direct from Yan Press. £10.99.

Morecambe Bay Solves the Heysham Mysteries. Robert Swain.
Yan Press ISBN 978-0-9540713-1-8

Travel back in time to discover why there are St. Peter's Church and St. Patrick's Chapel with its stone coffins side by side at Heysham. Discover how Morecambe Bay was a major influence.

This book explores the countryside, history, geology and folklore around Morecambe Bay in arriving at the solution.

Available from good bookshops and direct from Yan Press. £8.99.

MORECAMBE BAY RAMBLES